THE DANCING DEMOCRACY

When the Seven Party Alliance called for a four-day strike starting from 6 April 2006, the anniversary of Nepal's 1990 Jana Andolan, no one could have foreseen what would ensue. The protests brought hundreds of thousands on the streets, and finally resulted in a victory for the proletariat and democracy. As history is being made in Nepal, Prakash A. Raj takes a look at the main actors on the country's political stage — the monarch, the political parties, the Maoists, the international community — and analyses what happened in Nepal and why. He probes such questions as whether Nepal will become a republic or a ceremonial monarchy, who will control the Royal Nepalese Army and whether the Maoists will join mainstream politics or will try and capture power. Interspersed with striking photographs of the demonstrations held recently in Nepal, this book is an insightful look into the turbulence in Nepal, and how the power of the people prevailed. A must-read for anyone interested in South Asian politics.

A well-known writer, Prakash A. Raj is the author of *Kay Gardeko? The Royal Massacre in Nepal.* He comes from the family of Nepal's Royal Preceptors and his association with the ruling family dates back to the period of King Mahendra. Having studied and worked both in his country and abroad, he currently lives in Nepal.

D1733459

THE DANCING DEMOCRACY

The Power of the Third Eye

Prakash A. Raj

Cover and inside photographs by
Min Bajracharya

Rupa & Co

Typeset in Nikita Overseas Pvt. Ltd.
1410 Chiranjiv Tower
43 Nehru Place
New Delhi 110 019

Printed and bound in India by
Gopsons Papers Ltd., Noida.

Contents

Foreword

No period in the history of Nepal has been as tumultuous as the five years following the Royal massacre in June 2001, which resulted in the deaths of King Birendra, Queen Aishwarya, Prince Nirajan and six relatives of the royal family. Crown Prince Dipendra, the alleged assassin, was crowned while still in a coma, and died two days later. Following this tragedy, the democratic process in Nepal — as outlined in the 1990 Constitution, adopted after the Jana Andolan, People's Movement — began to be severely impeded. Sher Bahadur Deuba, elected prime minister under the parliamentary system by a party with the support of a majority of the members in the House of Representatives, was dismissed by King Gyanendra as being 'incompetent' in October 2002. In actuality, the prime minister had no right to continue in office after his inability to hold elections for Parliament within six months after he had recommended its dissolution.

There was a vacuum after Deuba's dismissal, and King Gyanendra exercised the powers of a prime minister. There was an erosion in public support for all three major institutions in the country: the monarch, political parties and the Maoists. That their monarch — considered an incarnation of Lord Vishnu — had been brutally murdered, allegedly by the Crown Prince, had shocked the Nepalese people. The monarchy had always been looked upon with respect; the institution had stayed clear of controversy for more than a decade after 1990 when the Panchayat system of government came to an end and sovereignty was transferred to the people and executive powers passed to a prime minister elected by a House of Representatives. Now, however, it became increasingly a target for criticism after Deuba was dismissed, criticism that began to spiral after February 2005 when the king formed a government under his chairmanship.

Political parties post-2001 were characterised by internal fighting, a lust for power, politicisation of bureaucracy and intelligence network, which led to a rapid spread of insurgency and corruption. While the Maoist insurgency, which started in 1996, had enjoyed some support in its initial years since it professed to be against corruption and bad governance, the public soon saw it as a force to be feared as it became increasingly violent. Maoist insurgents attacked many police posts, district headquarters and army barracks in this period but could not claim to control even a single town. This was in spite of the claims made not only by the insurgents but also independent observers that the insurgents controlled large areas in rural Nepal — perhaps as much as fifty percent of its total area. The Maoists called for strikes — 'Nepal Bandha' — frequently, crippling life all over the country. They even blockaded Kathmandu valley for a few weeks. According to Human Rights Watch, a Washington-based human rights group, Nepal has the largest number of 'disappeared persons' in the world; these 'disappeared persons' include people detained both by the state and Maoist insurgents.[1]

Both India and the US stopped their supply of arms to the Royal Nepalese Army after the royal takeover in 1 February 2005. The supply would be resumed, they said, after restoration of democracy by the monarch. A twelve-point accord was signed between seven agitating parties and the Maoists in New Delhi in November 2005. It appeared as if the political parties and the Maoists were on one side and the monarch and the government on the other. Despite the optimism surrounding the signing of the accord, however, there were serious doubts whether the Maoists would accept multi-party democracy and whether they would, in fact, surrender their arms before elections.

By April 2006, it appeared as if the situation in Nepal was still extremely fluid. Maoist insurgents were in control of much of the rural areas in the country. As Nepal's neighbours closely monitored events in Nepal, an alliance of seven political parties initiated a movement against autocratic monarchy on 6 April 2006, exactly sixteen years after the first Jana Andolan, which led to the transfer of sovereignty to the people of Nepal and the drafting of a new Constitution. Two weeks later it appeared as if the movement had gained widespread, vociferous support in Nepal. The royal government started to suppress the Jana Andolan with brutal measures that did not seem to succeed. At the time of writing,

---

1. *The Kathmandu Post*, 19 January '06.

it appears that the days of absolute monarchy in Nepal are numbered. However, it is still not clear what the outcome will be at this stage. Will Nepal become a republic? Or will there still be a ceremonial monarchy?

This book attempts to examine the roles of the three main actors on the Nepalese political stage, the monarch, the political parties and the Maoist insurgents, as well as that of the international community, including India, China and the United States of America. The stakes for India, Nepal's closest neighbour, are especially high keeping in mind security issues. Nepal's future, then, appears to lie in the outcome of the interaction between the three main actors internally, and the three external influences.

Kathmandu   Prakash A. Raj
April 2006

1

The Monarch:
An Incarnation of Vishnu?

> *'A Hindu king can't be under a Constitution.*
> *He is a part of God.'*
> Bharat Keshar Simha, retd. general, Royal Nepal Army,
> former ambassador to Britain (*Nepal Samacharpatra*, 24 June 2005)

> *'Traditional monarchy in Nepal ended with the Royal Massacre.'*
> Prachanda, Maoist Supreme Leader (*Dishabodh*, July 2001)

> *'In five years' time the King will either be executed by the*
> *people's court or maybe exiled.'*
> Prachanda in his interview with BBC
> (February 2006, cited in *The Telegraph* 22 February 2006)

On the stage that is Nepal's current political situation, King Gyanendra is without doubt the principal actor. When Nepal's monarch grabbed absolute power on 1 February 2005, political parties had ruled the country for more than a decade; a decade in which Maoist insurgents were able to grow from an insignificant Communist party, to one of the three main actors in Nepal.

Nepal is the only Hindu kingdom in the world, and King Gyanendra the only Hindu monarch of a sovereign independent country. It was believed, till as late as the mid-twentieth century, that the king was an incarnation of Lord Vishnu. If one saw the king on a particular day, it was thought, all the sins you might have committed on that day would be erased. In a country that is as multi-ethnic and multi-cultural as Nepal, the monarch was a symbol of national unity revered by all.

It was King Prithvi Narayan Shah of Gorkha who started the process of the unification of Nepal when he conquered the city state of Kathmandu in 1768. Nepal was then divided into about fifty small kingdoms and principalities. Over the years, King Prithvi Narayan Shah and his successors unified these kingdoms. In the mid-nineteenth century Jung Bahadur Rana became Nepal's first prime minister to wield absolute power. Rana set up an absolute oligarchy and the Shah kings were mere figureheads. For more than a century, from 1846 to 1950, the oligarchy ruled, till 1951, when the Rana regime was overthrown by a democracy movement. King Tribhuwan, Gyanendra's grandfather, who had taken asylum in India, returned to Nepal triumphantly in February 1951. His arrival marked the advent of democracy in Nepal. He declared that elections for a constitutional assembly would be held; this assembly would draft a Constitution for Nepal. However, he died in Zurich in 1955 before this could be accomplished.

King Tribhuwan's son Mahendra, who succeeded him, did not form a Constituent Assembly as his father had envisaged; instead he asked experts, including Sir Ivor Jennings from Britain, to frame a Constitution. This 1959 Constitution allowed for a Parliament to be elected on the basis of universal suffrage, and a Cabinet and prime minister responsible to the House. However, sovereignty rested with the king, and not with the people.

In 1958, elections for Parliament were held and B.P. Koirala — elder brother of Girija Koirala who was elected prime minister in 1991 — was elected prime minister.

King Gyanendra was crowned as the tenth monarch of the Shah dynasty in June 2001; in fact, it was the second time in fifty years that he had been crowned. Each time, he was third in line for the throne and an unlikely candidate for succession. The first time he was crowned was in 1950, when he was barely four years old. His grandfather, King Tribhuwan, his father, the then Crown Prince Mahendra and his elder brother, Prince Birendra, were at the time all in exile in India. Rana Prime Minister Mohan Shamsher declared Gyanendra to be the monarch at the time, as he was next in line to the throne. This crowning was not internationally recognised. The four-year-old's reign lasted less than three months. The Ranas conceded power soon after, and King Tribhuwan returned to Nepal along with his family.

King Gyanendra was again third in line for the throne before he was crowned in 2001: his elder brother King Birendra had two sons, Crown Prince Dipendra and Prince Nirajan, who superseded him. King Birendra and Prince Nirajan were assassinated, along with Queen Aishwarya and six other relatives, in June 2001, allegedly by Crown Prince Dipendra. The Crown Prince, who allegedly tried to kill himself after the shooting, was declared king while still in a coma. He died two days later and his uncle, Gyanendra, was declared king on 4 June 2001.

At the time of the king's ascension, Girija Prasad Koirala was prime minister, and there was a functioning parliamentary democracy in the country. Perhaps King Gyanendra's style of functioning was apparent from the minute his brother was assassinated. Although Koirala was executive head and, as such, should have been given full charge in a crisis, the prime minister was told — two hours after the actual incident — that the king had suffered a heart attack. He only learnt the truth when he reached the hospital.

Koirala later resigned, and was succeeded by Sher Bahadur Deuba who was to play a role in handing power to the king by dissolving Parliament and calling for elections that could not be held.[1]

Dismissal of Prime Minister Deuba

In October 2002, King Gyanendra, following in his father's footsteps, dismissed a prime minister elected by the majority party in Parliament. King Mahendra had, in 1960, similarly dismissed B.P. Koirala, elected by Nepali Congress Party in Parliament. However, there was one major difference between the two dismissals: King Mahendra still had full sovereignty

---

1. Shrestha, Aditya Man, 'Royal Massacre in Nepal: A Lingering Mystery', *Nepal Tomorrow: Voices and Visions*, Koselee Prakashan, Kathmandu, 2003.

under the 1959 Constitution; under the 1990 Constitution however, drafted after the People's Movement, sovereignty had been transferred to the people of Nepal.

King Gyanendra dismissed Deuba on charges of incompetence. Sher Bahadur Deuba had recommended that the House of Representatives be dissolved. It is mandatory to hold elections for the House of Representatives within six months of such dissolution. As Deuba was unable to hold such elections, primarily because of the Maoist insurgency, the king dismissed him, charging him with incompetence. King Gyanendra used Article 127 of the 1990 Constitution, which gave him powers to 'remove obstacles in the functioning of the Constitution'.

After Deuba's dismissal, the king invited leaders of political parties to form a ministry and appointed Lokendra Bahadur Chand and later Surya Bahadur Thapa as prime ministers. Both Chand and Thapa had been prime ministers during the Panchayat era before 1990 and both had served as prime ministers in coalition governments in the era of multi-party democracy in the period 1990-2002. Surya Bahadur Thapa had also been prime minister during King Mahendra's reign forty years earlier. After dismissing Surya Bahadur Thapa, King Gyanendra appointed Sher Bahadur Deuba again as prime minister. His Cabinet included several leaders of CPN (UML), including Bharat Mohan Adhikari as deputy prime minister.

The Royal Takeover

On 1 February 2005, King Gyanendra again used Article 127 to dismiss Deuba for the second time. He went on to form a Cabinet under his own chairmanship. In the royal proclamation he said no serious efforts had been made to initiate elections in the preceding year. He was also critical of the political parties; he said not a single House of Representatives had been allowed to complete its tenure during the multi-party era. He was also critical of the Maoist insurgents, who, he said, were murdering dissenters, kidnapping students and destroying projects aimed at people's welfare.[2] He also said that sovereignty in Nepal was vested in the people of Nepal and that only a successful multi-party democracy was synonymous with people's democracy. The king added that he and the Council of Ministers would give priority to re-activating multi-party democracy in the country within three years.

The dismissed prime minister, Sher Bahadur Deuba, was arrested a few days later at midnight, and charges against him were filed at the newly formed Royal Commission for Corruption Control (RCCC), set up to expedite corruption cases. Actually, one of the important features of multi-party rule between the years 1990 to 2002 was the pervasiveness of corruption in all echelons of government. Pokhrel Bharat in his article "Commissions, Kickbacks and Bribes in Nepal"[3] has written: 'Since 1990, all previous records of corruption have been broken as far as scale, categories, the status and number of personalities involved were concerned'. He cites an example of 'infamous political horse trading in 1996-97

---

2. Royal Proclamation, Annual Journal, 2004-5 Nepal Council of World Affairs.
3. *Nepal Tomorrow-Voices and Visions*, Koselee Prakashan, Kathmandu, 2003.

when parliamentarians were presenting themselves as a saleable commodity who were whisked away to Bangkok at public expense for "medical treatment" not at any hospital or clinic but at the massage parlours of the Thai capital'. Pokhrel concluded: 'As a result of several scams insidiously hatched by leaders belonging to most of the political parties, the poor kingdom has been recurrently swindled to the point of bankruptcy'.

Deuba's actions created a situation that enabled the king to take over. He was rumoured to be pro-palace as he was related to the king. Deuba's wife, Arzu Rana Deuba, is the great granddaughter of Rana Prime Minister Juddha Shamsher; Shamsher is also the great grandfather of King Gyanendra, from his mother's side of the family. Many people were surprised that Deuba was arrested.

Actually, there already existed, within the framework of the 1990 Constitution, a body set up to investigate abuses of power: the Commission for Investigation of Abuse of Authority (CIAA). Despite the existence of this body, the king formed the Royal Commission, stating that it would take swift action against corrupt politicians and officials. Deuba and a senior minister in his Cabinet, Prakash Man Singh, the son of freedom fighter Ganesh Man Singh, were arrested and charged with corruption in the Melamchi Drinking Water Project, which had been set up to alleviate the drinking water shortage in the Kathmandu valley. However, the Supreme Court declared the Royal Commission to be unconstitutional and it was disbanded in February 2006, a year after its formation, and Deuba was released. It is difficult to understand why King Gyanendra decided to form a new commission to take action against corrupt leaders and officials, when there was already a similar Constitutional body existing.

The United States has been relatively critical of the Maoists. However, it was also critical of the Royal takeover and the kind of ministers who were included in the Cabinet under the king's chairmanship. American Ambassador to Nepal James F. Moriarty had this to say: 'How can the government say it is serious about fighting corruption when it wilfully ignores the Asian Development Bank's (ADB) own report regarding the alleged corruption by former Prime Minister Deuba? How can the government say it is operating with good governance under the rule of law when the extra judicial RCCC's recent verdict looks more like a political vendetta than a serious exercise of judicial authority and when people who exercise their constitutional right to freedom of expression are imprisoned for sedition? Six months after the imposition of direct rule on February 1, with a questionable Cabinet full of Panchayat-era politicians and even a convicted criminal, the government seems to have gone back on its own core principles.'[4]

Monarchy, as an institution, suffered erosion in its support base after the Royal takeover in 2005. Even parties such as Nepali Congress and Nepali Congress (Democratic) — both of which had previously supported 'constitutional monarchy' in their party manifesto — have now declared that they are neutral as far as this institution is concerned.

The word for democracy in Nepali is 'prajatantra'; 'praja' means 'subject'. There was a slogan during the time of the

---

4. Address by American Ambassador James F. Moriarty to Nepal Council of World Affairs on 9 August '05.

Jana Andolan that said 'Praja hoina nagarik banaun' meaning 'Let's be citizens and not subjects'. Some politicians felt that the use of this word in the Nepalese context was relevant only if Nepal were to remain a kingdom. Many politicians started using another Sanskrit-based word 'Loktantra', 'lok' meaning people. This is also the Hindi word used for democracy in India. Some Maoists in Nepal use the word 'Janatantra' to signify 'people's republic'. The Maoists had supported the removal of the word 'His Majesty' ('Shree Panch', in Nepali) from 'His Majesty's Government' in offices in Dang and Piuthan in Rapti Zone — insurgency-affected areas.[5]

Meanwhile, the king had started visiting all five regions of the country to see for himself the prevailing situation. Many of these areas were affected by insurgency. He walked along town streets, visited army headquarters and administrative offices; some have written that he coerced the government into organising public felicitations.

From October 2002, Nepal had been ruled by ordinances as there was no Parliament where legislation approval could be granted, including budget and audit reports. The royal government had no accountability. However, between October 2002 and February 2005, there was at least the appearance of the king sharing power with political parties.[6] This façade was dropped when he took over completely on 1 February 2005. King Gyanendra had expressed his desire to be a 'constructive monarch' implying that he was not satisfied with the role given to the king under the 1990 Constitution.

---

5. Jana Astha, 12 April '06.
6. Ghimire, Yubaraj, 'Great Gambler', The Indian Express, 29 January '06.

Maoist Ceasefire (September–January 2005)

In September 2005, the Maoists announced a three-month unilateral ceasefire in an effort to aid talks with political parties. It was extended for an additional month in December. The announcement was welcomed by many political leaders in Nepal and by several foreign countries. India welcomed it as well; the official statement was that the move would pave the way for peace.[7] The secretary general of the United Nations urged all sides to take steps to begin peace talks.[8] The European Union asked the government to respond positively.[9] The Royal Nepalese Army, on the other hand, dismissed the Maoist unilateral ceasefire as a mere show and announced that it would continue operations against the Maoists.[10]

When the Maoists broke the ceasefire in January, they continued their attacks against district headquarters. The most significant was their attack in Tansen in Palpa district in the western hills and Dhankuta in the eastern hills that are situated in hillocks in defensive positions. The Maoists were successful in attacking both towns and took government officials as hostages. It was significant that both these towns had been the regional headquarters for hills west and east of Kathmandu during the Rana regime for more than a century.

---

7. *The Kathmandu Post*, 8 September '05.
8. Shrestha, Aditya Man, *The Himalayan Times*, 21 February '06.
9. *The Kathmandu Post*, 8 September '05.
10. *The Kathmandu Post* 9 September '05.

2

The Political Parties

Nepal was governed under the Panchayat system from 1961 to 1990. Under this system, political parties were banned, the monarch was sovereign and the prime minister and the council of ministers were responsible to him and not to the legislature. This was called the Rashtriya Panchayat. The most important achievements of the Popular Movement in 1990 was the transfer of sovereignty from the monarch to the people, the end of a party-less Panchayat system, and the establishment of multi-party democracy.

The Constitution promulgated in 1990 determined multi-party polity as an unalterable feature in the same way as Constitutional monarchy. An interim government — including representatives of the Nepali Congress, the Left and royalists — was formed in April 1990 with Krishna Prasad Bhattarai as prime minister.

Elections for Parliament were held in 1991 and the Nepali Congress won the majority of seats, followed by CPN (UML). While the Nepali Congress could be considered as a 'social democratic' party, the CPN (UML) represented moderate Left and was a Communist party that believed in the multiparty system. The Rashtriya Prajatantra Party (RPP), which included many politicians from the Panchayat system, was the third largest party in the House of Representatives. The Nepal Sadbhavana Party, representing some constituencies in the Terai, also won a few seats. A government headed by Girija Prasad Koirala, the younger brother of B.P. Koirala, the first elected prime minister of Nepal, was formed. However, the Parliament was dissolved before completing its term in July 1994.

The 1994 general elections produced a fractured verdict and the CPN (UML) emerged as the party with the largest number of seats in Parliament. Manmohan Adhikari was appointed prime minister in November 1994, the first ever Communist to hold such a post in a monarchy. He dissolved Parliament and called for elections. However, the Supreme Court overturned the decision and the Parliament was resurrected. He was voted out after being in power for only nine months. A series of coalition governments followed, headed by several prime ministers including those from RPP. Elections to Parliament in 1999 led to the Nepali Congress getting a majority of seats, and Girija Prasad Koirala being instated as prime minister.

In 2001, King Gyanendra ascended the throne and Nepal was a Constitutional monarchy, with a prime minister who enjoyed the confidence of a majority of members in Parliament till October 2002. Sher Bahadur Deuba became the new prime minister replacing Koirala. He dissolved the Parliament in May 2002 and called for elections. According to the 1990 Constitution, elections would need to be held within six months of the Parliament being dissolved. However, Deuba was unable to do so primarily because of the Maoist insurgency in the country, and King Gyanendra dismissed him.

It is interesting to note that all the major political parties in the country — Nepali Congress, CPN (UML), RPP and Sadbhavana — have split post 1990. The Nepali Congress split into the Nepali Congress headed by Girija Prasad Koirala and Nepali Congress (Democratic) headed by Sher Bahadur Deuba. There was a centrifugal tendency in the party since the formation of the first government as there was a group of members who opposed Koirala. Similarly, the CPN (ML) separated from CPN (UML) and later re-united. The RPP split into factions headed by Surya Bahadur Thapa and Lokendra Bahadur Chand. In 1996, Surya Bahadur Thapa created a new party named Rashtriya Janshakti Party. There are now two factions of Nepal Sadbhavana Party, one of which — headed by Badri Mandal — supported the Royal takeover in February 2005, and the other — headed by Anandi Devi — has been opposed to the takeover and is part of the Seven Party Alliance.

It was suggested that, 'The power struggles between the G.P. Koirala and K.P. Bhattarai / Sher Bahadur Deuba factions within the Nepali Congress, and the Madhav Nepal and K.P. Oli factions in the post-divided UML has dominated Nepali politics. This has been a main cause of political instability, lack of effective governance, erosion of norms, values and the pervasive corruption that have characterised post 1990 governments in Nepal'.[1]

In 2002, the Nepali Congress had been the ruling party in ten of the twelve years of the post-Panchayat system period, and Girija Prasad Koirala had been the prime minister for the longest period during his party's rule. A recent study found that the support base of both major parties NC and UML had eroded, with both parties relying more on money, power and patronage instead of contributing to development activities. They now lacked clear vision. The study concluded that both parties were showing a trend as protectors of a 'status quo' rather than being agents of change.[2]

Twelve-Point Seven Party-Maoist Agreement

A watershed event occurred on 22 November 2005, when a Twelve-Point Accord was signed between the Maoists and seven political parties agitating for an end to what they called 'autocratic monarchy'.

Before 2005, political parties and the monarch were together in trying to fight the Maoist movement. However, the situation was to change dramatically. Seven major political parties signed an agreement with the Maoists, with the aim being an end to autocratic monarchy and elections to a Constituent Assembly. It was, for all practical purposes, an

1. *Enabling State Program*, pro-poor governance assessment in Nepal 2001, Kathmandu.
2. Hathechhu, Krishna in *Nepali Politics: People-Parties Interface, Resistance and the State: Nepalese Experiences*, edited by David Gellner, Social Science Press, Delhi.

accord to end monarchy in Nepal and turn it into a republic. One columnist has said this agreement became necessary because, 'Humiliated and marginalised, the political parties' leaders had no other option but to strike a deal for mounting a mass struggle against the rise of royal absolutism'.[3] American Ambassador James F. Moriarty said a major share of blame for the Twelve-Point Understanding between the Seven Party Alliance and the Maoists should go to the king, who didn't give 'any other option to the parties'.[4]

The seven parties signing the agreement were as follows:

1. Nepali Congress
2. Nepali Congress (Democratic)
3. Nepal Sadbhavana Party (Anandi Devi faction)
4. CPN (United Marxist Leninist)
5. Samyukta Jan Morcha (United People's Front)
6. Nepal Peasant's and Worker's Party
7. United Leftist Front

The first three parties are non-Communist. While Nepali Congress and Nepali Congress (Democratic) have a following all over Nepal, NSP's influence is largely restricted to the Terai. The UML has a strong support base all over the country and is the largest Communist party that could be considered moderate Left. Nepal Peasants and Workers Party's influence is limited to Bhaktapur district. The SJM represents the radical Left and its ideology is similar to that of the Maoists. The United Left Front consists of a cluster of small Communist

3. Baral, Lok Raj, *The Himalayan Times*, 27 March '06.
4. *The Kathmandu Post*, 27 February '06.

parties with limited influence. About ninety percent of the seats in the dissolved Parliament belonged to these seven parties. The RPP, which includes many politicians who were active during the Panchayat era, its offshoots and one faction of NSP headed by Badri Prasad Mandal are not part of the agitating alliance. Such small parties as Nepal Samata Party and Nepal Green Party did not have a single member in Parliament.

The Twelve-Point Agreement was signed in New Delhi presumably with the tacit consent of the Government of India. The salient features of the agreement are as follows:

a) An autocratic monarchy is the main obstacle, and peace and prosperity is impossible without ending 'autocracy' and establishing 'absolute democracy'.

b) Re-instatement of Parliament dissolved in 2002 and formation of an interim government followed by elections to a Constituent Assembly.

c) Supervision of the arms of the Royal Nepal Army and the Maoists by the UN or other international bodies to ensure free and fair elections to the Constituent Assembly.

d) Acceptance of multi-party competition, fundamental rights of people, human rights, rule of law and democratic principles and values by CPN (Maoist).

e) CPN (M) will allow leaders and cadres affiliated to other 'democratic forces' to return to their respective places with respect, and will return houses and properties that have been seized. Displaced people will be similarly allowed to return home and will be allowed to engage in political activities.

f) CPN (M) agrees to self-criticism for past mistakes and agrees not to repeat them in the future.

g) The parties will consider their own mistakes and will not repeat them in the future.

h) During the peace process, human rights principles and freedom of the Press will be fully respected.

i) The municipal and Parliamentary elections will be boycotted.

j) Appeal by the Seven Party Alliance and the Maoists to the Nepali people and the international community to support their democratic movement and to oppose those who support the monarchy and their brand of nationalism.

k) Appeal by Seven Party Alliance and the Maoists to civil society members and organisations and professionals to support their 'People's Peaceful Movement'.

l) Seven Party Alliance agree to probe into past incidents and take action against the guilty. Future problems among political parties to be settled through dialogue among 'high-level leaders'.

Several of the points in the agreement could perhaps be questioned regarding their legality. For instance, the second point calls for the re-instatement of the Parliament dissolved in 2002. However, neither the Maoists nor the political parties have the authority to ask for the re-instatement of a dissolved Parliament or for elections to a Constituent Assembly. This is because they are not sovereign bodies. As sovereignty was transferred to the people in 1990, only an elected Parliament can decide whether to call for elections to a Constituent Assembly or amend the existing Constitution.

James F. Moriarty has said that he does not see a future for Nepal if the parties do go ahead with their Twelve-Point Agreement with the rebels. He has asked such Constitutional forces as the king and the political parties to reconcile. Moriarty has been critical of the Royal takeover and has said more than 'twelve months of palace rule have only made the situation more precarious and emboldened the Maoist insurgents'.[5]

Maoist leader Babu Ram Bhattarai, while replying to the US's concern about the agreement, wrote that, contradictory to Moriarty's charges, the CPN (Maoist) was not a totalitarian party. He has accused Moriarty of a McCarthy-ian mindset, as the historic resolution passed on 'Development of Democracy in the 21st Century' had affirmed Maoist commitment to multi-party competitive politics in the future republic of Nepal.[6]

Maoist Supreme Leader Prachanda has proposed to the political parties that they form a parallel government and a common army including PLA and cadres from SPA. He said he would also favour monarchy if the people voted in favour of the institution and the elected Constituent Assembly approved. Both Prachanda and Babu Ram Bhattarai have said they will not accept any political post, such as president or prime minister, even if their party were to come to power in the future. They would spend their time 'educating the younger generation'.[7]

A Nepalese professor of International Law at the University of Leeds thinks a parallel government, as suggested by the Maoists, would have its own legal and political issues

---

5. *The Kathmandu Post*, 16 February '06.
6. Bhattarai, Babu Ram, 'On Moriarty's Pontification', *The Kathmandu Post*, 23 February '06.
7. Interview with Prachanda, *Kantipur*, 7 February '06.

and might further compound the problems of the country. He believes, 'It will be difficult to recognise a parallel government which does not exercise a meaningful and effective control of a territory within the country', as in the case of Nepal at the present time. The US and the UK would not recognise any government backed or led by the Maoists under the present situation, he feels.[8]

A professor at Tufts University, US — analysing the political history of Nepal and predicting the future scenario of the country — has said he believes the king will be forced to flee, like the Shah, Marcos and Mobuto before him. The SPA and the Maoists will be unable to come to an agreement on what the next step should be, and a leader of the Nepali Congress will most probably head a provisional government. The SPA will want disarmament of the Maoists and RNA while re-instating the dissolved Parliament. The Maoists might want a national conference before disarming. Down the line, dissatisfaction with the provisional government and the likely slow pace of change will result in a second urban uprising led by the Maoists and supported by the SPA. The professor believes that the urban uprising from the Russian model will meet the Chinese model characterised by control of rural areas by Maoists, which will result in Nepal becoming largely Communist.[9]

8. Subedi, Surya P., 'Resolving Political Crisis', *The Kathmandu Post*, 6 March '06.
9. Leupp, Gary, 'Nepal Pact', *Counterpunch*, 27 November '05.

3

The Maoists

'The Maoist movement is for liberation for exploited, oppressed, women, Dalits, Janjats and those who have remained weak.'
Babu Ram Bhattarai, *Nepal*, 9 April 2006

Nepal was known as a peaceful country, the birthplace of Buddha, a Shangri-la for tourists, home of eight out of the ten highest peaks in the world including Mount Everest. It had never been conquered by an outsider, nor colonised, unlike other countries in South Asia. It was a multi-lingual, multi-ethnic country united by a Hindu king. Both Mahayana and Vajrayana Buddhism co-existed peacefully with Hinduism.

Nepal enjoys another distinction now. At a time when Communism ended in the Soviet Union and Eastern Europe, Nepal began to be affected by the Maoist movement. It is now estimated — a decade after the insurgency began — that 15,000 persons have lost their lives in the violence.

In 2002, the prime minister dissolved the Parliament. Because of the violence caused by Maoist insurgents, elections could not be held, as they should have been, within six months of the dissolution. King Gyanendra appointed himself chairman of the Council of Ministers, and since then, legislations are brought into effect by ordinances that are valid for six months. As there has been no Parliament in the country since 2002, the country's budget is also brought about by ordinance. In other words, there is no democracy in the country.

In February 2006, elections for municipal bodies were held, but all the major political parties boycotted it, while the Maoists threatened candidates.

The Maoist insurgency had its beginnings in February 1996. The Maoist party, CPN (Maoist), had presented a Forty-Point demand list to Prime Minister Sher Bahadur Deuba, most of which seemed reasonable. However, the prime minister chose not to pay any attention to the demands.

The ultimate objective of the Maoist insurgency is that a People's Republic is formed in Nepal, and monarchy abolished. The Maoists say that the legacy of discrimination, which began in 1768 when unification started in Nepal, can be changed only by revolution. They are in favour of making Nepal a secular state. They want a new Constitution formed by a Constituent Assembly that is elected by the people.

Effects of the Insurgency

- Migration from rural to urban areas and to foreign countries has increased. Depopulation of many villages in the western hills has been noticed. A large number of the Nepalese now work in the Gulf and Malaysia and bring US$ 1 billion annually as remittances, which has saved the economy from collapsing.
- Schoolchildren, some as young as fourteen, are being forcibly recruited to the Maoist Army. The Maoists reportedly force each family to send at least one person to join their army.
- Schools teaching Sanskrit have been closed.
- Rural areas in fifty out of seventy-five districts, mainly in the western hills, are under Maoist control. The figures may be somewhat exaggerated, but the presence of the government in the rural areas of the country is minimal.
- Maoists have their own tax system in the areas under their control. They have imposed taxes on businesses and salaried classes. It is reported that businesses in urban areas, including Kathmandu, pay taxes to them for their own security. Some businesses have been allegedly attacked because of their failure to pay taxes to the Maoists. The teachers in schools in the rural areas have been especially hard hit, as their remuneration is meagre, and they are required to pay ten to fifteen percent of their salary as taxes to the Maoists. Foreigners who travel to the areas along the Everest and Annapurna, have to pay taxes amounting to US $15 to 50 to the Maoists.
- The Maoists have their own justice system, including a 'People's Court'. Most of those punished are put in Maoist

'labour camps' where they are made to work. The Maoists have also introduced their own 'visa' system in areas controlled by them.

- The Maoists have also formed nine 'autonomous areas' based on the ethnicity in different parts of the country. These include Magarat in mid-western and western hills containing a large number of Magars, Tamuwan in Gandaki zone around Pokhara, and Tharuwan in western Terai. However, almost all the autonomous areas are multi-ethnic; no ethnic group forms a majority of the population. A Cabinet of Magarat Autonomous Region stretching from Palpa to Rukum announced Santosh Budha Magar as its 'chief minister' recently. The formation of a 135-member People's Representative Assembly and approval of a three-year budget amounting to Rs 200.5 million was also announced.[1]

- Maoists have also been involved in the destruction of development infrastructure such as building of local government, telecommunication towers and bridges throughout the country.

- Widespread human rights abuses from both the Maoists and the Nepal army have been noted.

- The number of tourists visiting Nepal has declined.

Socio-Economic Impact of Maoist Insurgency

- High caste widows, who traditionally wore white, have now begun to wear red. Some old values are being questioned.

1. *Jana Astha*, 5 April '05.

- As a large number of conscripts in the Maoist army have been women (perhaps as much as forty percent), the Royal Nepal Army has also started recruiting women.
- Many people blame misrule by political parties between 1990 and 2002, widespread corruption and politicisation of police and intelligence network for the rise of the Maoist insurgency. Political parties have suffered a loss of popularity and credibility. There is no doubt that the security system in the country was better before 1990, although the country didn't have a multi-party democracy and only a limited amount of freedom of expression and assembly.
- Need for affirmative action or reservation for Dalits, women and Janjatis is now widely accepted.
- Calls for strikes or 'Nepal Banda' and forcible closure of educational institutions has affected education for all and damaged the economy.

Recent Developments (2006)

- The Maoists have not been able to capture a single district headquarters.
- The security situation in Kathmandu valley had initially improved after the Royal takeover. For a time, in the beginning of 2005, Kathmandu valley itself seemed vulnerable. However, after calls for strikes made by SPA and the curfew imposed by the government in the first two weeks of April 2006, the situation has worsened. There was widespread defiance of the curfew. However, it does not seem as if there has been much improvement outside the valley.

- India, the US and Britain, three major arms suppliers to Nepal suspended arms aid to Nepal after 1 February 2005 as a protest against the royal coup. India's role is crucial because of the open border between the two countries. The visa section of the American Embassy and the American Library were closed in April 2006 and non-essential diplomatic staff was advised to leave the country.
- In spite of suggestions by India, the US and Britain that the monarchy and political parties work together to defeat the Maoists, there has been no progress. Two 'talks' between the government and the Maoists in 2001 and 2003 failed with the Maoists walking out. On the other hand, the government did not reciprocate the Maoists' four-month ceasefire between September 2005 and January 2006. Countries such as Norway and Switzerland and organisations such as the United Nations are interested in mediating between the government and the Maoists, if asked to do so, but it seems unlikely at present. The solution to the present crisis will require elections to either Parliament under the present Constitution, or to a Constituent Assembly, which will draft a new Constitution. No elections are possible as long as the Maoists are armed. A military solution on the part of the government will be extremely costly.
- In 2005, there were some protest movements against the Maoists in districts in the western hills and the Terai in 2005; however, the alliance between SPA and the Maoists in 2006 has resulted in an end to these protests.
- External forces are playing an increasing role. Maoists are members of RIM, an organisation that includes such movements as Shining Path in Peru and Naxalites in

India. Maoist leaders spend some time in India, which has its own Maoist problem in several states. The open Indo-Nepal border facilitates this.

• The UN has appointed a UNHCR representative in Nepal under Agenda Item 19 as agreed by Nepal in April 2005. By 2006 it had become one of the largest UN human rights monitoring bodies in operation anywhere. UNHCR has found several instances of human rights violations between September 2005 and January 2006 by both the state and the Maoists. The state has been found to have arrested, detained and re-arrested those suspected of being Maoists or sympathisers. Torture was also found to be pervasive. The UNHCR has also collected information about kidnapping, killing of security personnel and general public by the Maoists. There is concern that the Maoists are using a large number of child soldiers. Maoist leaders have said that it is not their policy to target families of state security forces or to kill unarmed security personnel, and action is being taken against perpetrators of these crimes. The displacement of a large population due to the conflict has also been recorded.[2]

• As mentioned before, seven political parties agitating against the royal government have, in November 2005, signed an agreement with the Maoists calling for elections to a Constituent Assembly to draft a new Constitution.

• Two top Maoist leaders, Rabindra Shrestha and Mani Thapa (Anukul), members of the Maoist Politbureau,

---

2. Report of UNHCR on the situation of human rights and the activities of the office, including technical cooperation, in Nepal.

rebelled against the leadership of the Party and made their grievances public in 2006. Rabindra Shrestha pointed out that Babu Ram Bhattarai was educating his child in a foreign country instead of being recruited in the People's Army. He charged Prachanda of nepotism and intellectual poverty. He has accused both Prachanda and Babu Ram of waging a 'People's War' living in a foreign country. Both Rabindra Shrestha and Mani Thapa were immediately expelled from CPN (Maoist). An article published in a monthly reportedly close to the Maoists, pointed out that children of several leaders other than Prachanda and Babu Ram — such as Bahadur Bogati, Agni Sapkota and Pasang — were either fighting or had been killed while participating in the insurgency.[3]

---

3. Shrestha, Ravindra, 'Janamukti Sena Maathi Prachanda ra Baburam ko Gaddari', *Nepal Samacharpatra*, 25 March '06; Dhital, Manarishi, 'Gahro chha aphnai bichalan chhopna', *Mulyankan* April 2006, Chait 2062.

4

April 2006: When the People Rose

When the Seven Party Alliance announced a four-day strike in Kathmandu valley, from 6-10 April 2006, few expected that it would result in a second Jana Andolan, let alone an *andolan* that would be even more powerful than the first. No one expected that the four days would extend to more than eighteen days, and shake the very foundations of the 237-year-old monarchy.

What started as a movement for ending 'regression', meaning the Royal takeover of 1 February 2005, had gathered momentum after the Seven Party Alliance had signed a Twelve-Point Agreement with the Maoists in November 2005. Although many of the leaders of the SPA had helped in the drafting of the 1990 Constitution, the agreement with the Maoists included one of the Maoists' principal demands: elections to a Constituent Assembly that would draft a new Constitution.

The four-day strike was announced to coincide with the anniversary of the Popular Movement or Jana Andolan of April 1990 which had resulted in a huge crowd marching to the Royal Palace and the proclamation by the king to disband the Panchayat system, set up multi-party democracy and to transfer sovereignty to the people. It appears that the widespread support for the 2006 Jana Andolan will result in even more dramatic changes, including a distinct possibility that Nepal could become a republic.

Just before the start of the strike, the People's War started by the Maoists had, in February 2006, celebrated its tenth anniversary. As the Maoists had signed a pact with the mainstream political parties comprising the SPA, they had also declared a ceasefire in their activities in the Kathmandu valley. However, they were still active elsewhere in the country. They had launched successful attacks in Tansen, Palpa in the western hills and Dhankuta in the eastern hills but didn't control a single district headquarters in the country. However, their area of influence included much of the rural area of the country. On the night of 6 April, the Maoists attacked Malangawa, the district headquarters of Sarlahi. A night vision helicopter sent to the site met with an accident. Seven soldiers belonging to the Royal Nepal Army, six policemen, five Maoists and some civilians were killed. Nine security men and the chief district officer were kidnapped by the Maoists, who set free 197 prisoners from the District Prison. While the Maoists say they shot down the helicopter using a mix of indigenous and scientific techniques (the Maoists had demonstrated such 'anti-aircraft' guns in western Terai one week earlier[1]), the RNA said it crashed due to technical difficulties.

1. Bhat, Bhojraj, 'Kasari Khasyo Helicopter', *Nepal*, 16 April '06.

The attack on Malangawa was significant as it was also the first ever such attack in the headquarters of a district in the Terai, close to the Indian border. The Communists in Nepal had limited influence in the Terai as such parties as Nepali Congress, Nepal Sadbhavana Party and RPP had won most of the seats there in all the parliamentary elections held since 1990. The attack showed that the Maoists had increased their influence there; they proposed the setting up of a 'Madhesh Autonomous Area' in eastern and central Terai, and a 'Tharuwan Autonomous Area' in western Terai.

A daytime curfew had to be imposed on 8 April in the cities of the Kathmandu valley in order to prevent the large demonstration that was being planned by the SPA to coincide with the day the 1990 Jana Andolan had emerged victorious. On the same day, the Maoists attacked Butwal, an important town in western Terai and a transport hub linking Kathmandu with the Indian border and Pokhara, situated along the East-West Highway. The small district headquarter town of Taulihawa was also attacked.

Curfew was re-imposed on 9, 10 and 11 April, and there was widespread defiance in the Kathmandu valley. The residents of the valley had not shown much support to the SPA's agitation, which had begun around October 2002. However, this seemed to have changed in some respects. Those areas where there were protests, were precisely those areas that have a large number of displaced persons from outside the valley, and who are relatively less affluent. There were also widespread demonstrations in towns outside the Kathmandu valley.

Although SPA had announced strikes only for four days in April, they had affirmed that it would continue indefinitely.

The Maoists, meanwhile, reiterated their support to the agitating SPA. By the third day of the protests, many professionals such as doctors, lawyers and engineers had joined. Employees of government-owned industries such as telecom, water and electricity supply boards and banks (including Nepal Bank) also supported the protest. The staff of the Nepal Rastra Bank, the country's central bank, kept the central treasury vault closed and did not conduct any transactions. Twelve staff members of Nepal Rastra Bank were later arrested by the police.

By the sixth day, the government had lifted the curfew as the situation had improved. However, the police opened fire at a poetry recital meeting in Old Baneshwar area of Kathmandu, where artists and journalists had gathered to watch a play. Some staff at the Ministry of Home Affairs stopped work to protest against this government atrocity, and to support the movement. It is customary for the King of Nepal to send a New Year message on the Nepali New Year Day on April 14. People expected that this year, the king would include an invitation for dialogue with leaders of the SPA and a proposal to end the confrontation. This was missing, however.

The strike began to affect Thamel, the tourist area of Kathmandu, by the tenth day. A procession of tourist entrepreneurs and some foreign tourists was attacked by the police. One British tourist was beaten up. Private banks that had remained open the first few days of the strike, were also ordered to close by the SPA. Uncollected garbage in the streets was piling up as the strikers had banned movement of all vehicles. All schools remained closed.

On the eleventh day, the SPA ordered all businesses not to pay taxes including VAT, to the government or charges for electricity, telephone and water. They also boycotted products produced by industries that were owned by the royal family.[2] The staff of government offices including the Home Ministry, the Cabinet Secretariat and Appellate and Supreme Courts also demonstrated and joined in the protests. It was reported by BBC that crowds numbering more than 100,000 demonstrated in such towns as Bhairawa, Nepalganj and Butwal. A columnist noted that the crowds included a large number of women, and of people between the ages of twelve and twenty-two.[3] It was rumoured that the Maoists had ordered each household in the valley and the surrounding districts to send at least one person to participate in the rally.

Karan Singh, the Indian prime minister's special envoy to Nepal, and India's Foreign Secretary Shyam Saran were sent by the Government of India to Nepal on 19 April. The reason why India chose Karan Singh could be due to his long association with Nepal and his marriage into the Rana family. Singh met leaders of political parties and had an audience with King Gyanendra, to whom he gave a message from Indian Prime Minister Dr. Manmohan Singh.

On 20 April, the SPA called for a huge demonstration and rally in Kathmandu. The government imposed a twenty-hour curfew inside the Ring Road. Around 200,000 people attended the demonstration. Many tried to defy curfew and enter the inner city from such locations as Kalanki, southwest and Gongabu and Balaju north of the city. The worst clash

2. *Kantipur*, 17 April '06.
3. Roka, 'Hari Kursika Lagi Hoina Janaandolan', *Kantipur*, 17 April '06.

between the security forces and the demonstrators took place in Kalanki, when three people were killed and 100 injured when they were fired on. A government revenue office was set on fire and the police and army did not intervene. The crowds managed to enter the inner city chanting anti-monarchy slogans.

On 21 April, King Gyanendra announced in a royal proclamation that he had agreed to transfer executive powers to the people and asked the SPA to recommend the name of a prime minister. Had the king made this announcement on the Nepali New Year Day, perhaps the people and the SPA would have welcomed it. But now, Nepal was on the brink of a revolution, and what the king was offering was too little, too late for the many protesters and, above all, the Maoists. Protests continued. Never before had the country seen more than one million people taking part in a demonstration.[4] The city was still under curfew, but defiant protesters entered the city centre area, chanting slogans against the king and burning his effigies.

Meanwhile, India, the US, European Union, Canada and China welcomed the royal proclamation. India's Foreign Secretary Shyam Saran, however, pointed out that this would not solve the political problem. This was different from what Karan Singh and National Security Advisor M.K. Narayanan had earlier said, which was that India supported constitutional monarchy in Nepal.

An estimated 200,000 persons joined the anti-monarchy protests in Dang district in western Nepal on 23 April. There were the first-ever protests in the trans-Himalayan districts

---

4. *Kantipur*, 22 April '06.

of Mustang and Manang by district level leaders.[5] The Maoists attacked the district headquarters of Sindhupalchok situated north of Kathmandu valley. They attacked RNA barracks and the telecom tower. A procession in Nepalganj city in the Terai vandalised the statue of King Tribhuwan. A historic palace in Besi Shahar of Lamjung district was vandalised by a mob that burnt all the photos of the Shah kings there and replaced signboards stating 'His Majesty's Government' with those saying 'Nepal Government'.[6] It appeared that the movement was becoming increasingly anti-monarch, rather than pro-democracy.

Fourteen persons died and five thousand were injured in the eighteen days of protests. The National Human Rights Commission expressed its view that excessive force was used by security forces against demonstrators by such means as bullets, teargas and lathi-charge without warning.[7]

---

5. *Gorkhapatra*, 24 April '06.
6. *The Kathmandu Post*, 24 April '06.
7. *Nepal Samacharpatra*, 24 April '06.

5

The Royal Nepal Army

'Today it is not the kingship but the RNA that is the country's most powerful institution.'
Dhruba Kumar, 'The Royal Nepali Army',
Himal Southasia, March-April 2006

'The main problem of Nepal is a feudal palace and the trained RNA that has been made loyal to this institution for the past two-and-a-half centuries.'
Prachanda, *Weekly Samaya*, 21 April 2006

The Royal Nepal Army was set up by the kings of Gorkha, in particular Prithvi Narayan Shah, who was responsible for the unification of Nepal. The most important event in the task of unification was the conquest of Kathmandu in 1768. This was completed during the regency of Queen Rajendralaxmi and Prince Bahadur Shah.

Greater Nepal, before the Ango-Gorkha War in 1814, extended from Tista in the east to Sutlej in the west. Leadership, bravery and motivation were all important factors that contributed to the success of the Nepalese army, then called the Gurkha Army. In the initial stages of unification, the army consisted largely of Chhetri, Thakuri, Magar and Gurung ethnic groups. Actually, Gurungs and Magars were the indigenous inhabitants of the Chaubisi area where the unification of Nepal started. The area also contained a large number of Bahuns, Chhetris and Dalits, whose first language was Nepali. The army came under the control of the Ranas after the Kot Massacre of 1846, when Jung Bahadur was appointed prime minister by Queen Rajya Laxmi, who had been granted sovereign powers by King Rajendra. It was to remain under the Rana oligarchy for more than a century till 1951.

In 1762, when Prithvi Narayan Shah imposed a blockade in the Kathmandu valley and conquered Makwanpur, Mir Qasim of Bengal attacked his forces in the Terai. The Gurkha army defeated his army by attacking at night; the confrontation resulted in 1,700 of Mir Qasim's army dying, and about 25 to 30 soldiers of the Gurkha army.

The king of Kathmandu valley, Jaya Prakash Malla, asked the British to help him against Prithvi Narayan Shah in 1767. Captain Kinlock was sent from Patna with 2,400 troops to help the king. The troops were defeated, however, in the battle of Sindhuli, and the lives of 1,600 men were lost. The Gurkha army also fought in Tibet in 1792 during the regency of

Bahadur Shah before 12,000 Chinese and Tibetan troops invaded Nepal from Keyrung. The Nepalese troops had to retreat and were followed by the Chinese. The Chinese army was defeated in Betrawati, fifty kilometres west of Kathmandu. This was the first time the Royal Nepal Army (RNA) had to fight the huge army of the Chinese.

The RNA was defeated in the Anglo-Nepal War of 1814-16; the soldiers fought with such valour, however, that even the opposing army praised them. Nepal lost a third of its territory after the Treaty of Sugauli. Nepal emerged victorious in the second Nepal-Tibet War in 1856.

The RNA was used by Jung Bahadur to help the British suppress the Indians during the First War of Independence in the Gangetic Plains in 1857. The British restored four western Terai districts of Banke, Bardia, Kailali and Kanchanpur that Nepal had lost during the Treaty of Sugauli.

The Ranas also provided 16,554 army men at the service of British Indian regiments during the First World War (1914-1919). It was reported that twenty battalions were sent from Kathmandu for this purpose.[1] Meanwhile, more than 200,000 Gurkhas were also being recruited directly for British Indian regiments. They fought in France, Mesopotamia, Palestine and Salonika. Four battalions of the RNA were sent to fight in the Third Afghan War in 1929. During the Second World War (1939-45), battalions from the RNA were sent in combat to the Indian subcontinent and elsewhere. The sixteen battalions fought in the Assam-Burma (the latter now known as Myanmar) sector in the east. Gurkha units of the Indian

---

1. Khatri, Tek Bahadur, Shahi Nepali Sena ko Itihas, Saharada Kumari KC, Kathmandu, BS 2041.

Army fought in Malaya, the Middle East, North Africa and Europe.

The last hereditary Rana prime minister of Nepal, Mohan Shamsher, sent ten battalions of RNA soldiers to help the government of independent India in 1948 to fight in Hyderabad and Kashmir. Resources of the Indian army were stretched to the maximum at the time, and help from Nepal must have provided aid at a crucial time.[2]

After the advent of democracy in Nepal in 1951, the army's loyalty shifted from the Ranas to the king. B.P. Koirala, the first elected prime minister of Nepal, who was also Home minister in the first Rana-Nepali Congress interim government under Prime Minister Mohan Shamsher Rana, has written in some detail about how it happened. The Rana prime ministers kept a loyal battalion of the Nepali army, called Bijuli Garat, which stayed in the barracks in Singha Durbar, the residence of the Rana prime ministers at that time. When Mohan Shamsher moved to his own residence after vacating Singha Durbar in 1951, a decision had to be taken regarding where the Bijuli Garat would go. B.P. Koirala suggested that the battalion be taken to the Royal palace. Babar Shamsher Rana, who was the commander-in-chief, had already left Nepal for Bangalore, India, on a self-imposed exile. Kiran Shamsher Rana was appointed deputy commander-in-chief. It was he who transferred Bijuli Garat from Singha Durbar to the Royal palace. The next morning, B.P. Koirala saw the Bijuli Garat saluting King Tribhuwan the same way it used to salute Mohan Shamsher Rana, without any prior instructions. 'It was from that day on that the King

2. Koirala, B.P., Atmabrittanta, *Jagadamba Prakashan*, BS 2055.

had the upper hand compared to democracy', Koirala writes. If Bijuli Garat had remained with Mohan Shamsher Rana, who had now become interim prime minister, Koirala felt they 'would have retained an important role. Once the army went to him, he [the King] became stronger'.[3]

When the elected government with B.P. Koirala as prime minister was dismissed by King Mahendra ten years later in December 1960, the coup succeeded because it had the support of the army. Koirala has written, 'If we had kept fifty Israeli sub-machine guns with us, they could not have done this to us'.[4] B.P. Koirala wrote an article about the RNA in a publication fifteen years after he was deposed, while he was living in exile in India. He wrote about how the soldiers in the RNA felt that the monarch was above the country. He pointed out that, instead of the army being called National Nepal Army, it had become the Royal Nepal Army. According to him, the army gave more importance to loyalty than to moral values or laws of the land and justice. He said a small faction of the army based at the Royal Palace was in control of the RNA. He was perhaps referring to the Military Secretariat of the Royal Palace, which, during the Panchayat era, was headed by General Sher Bahadur Malla and was very powerful. He suggested that the RNA be renamed the Nepal National Army and that troops stationed in the Royal Palace should be merged with the NNA.[5]

---

3. Ibid.
4. Koirala, B.P., 'Shahi Sena ko Lokatantrikaran', *Mulyankan*, April 2006, quoting Tarun Bulletin, 7 December 1975.
5. Mehta, Ashok, *Royal Nepal Army*, Rupa & Co, Delhi.

During the 1990 Jana Andolan, the RNA remained loyal to the king. A compromise was reached during the drafting of the 1990 Constitution, under which the king remained the supreme commander-in-chief with the power to appoint the COAS on the recommendation of the prime minister; a National Security Council, headed by the prime minister, would take charge over all military operations.[6]

B.P. Koirala was not the only one calling for people's control over the army. In their forty-point demand list submitted to Prime Minister Deuba, the Maoists also demanded that, 'The army, the police and the bureaucracy should be directly under people's control'.[7] As the police and bureaucracy were directly under the elected government, it is interesting to note that the Maoists did not then make a distinction about who controlled the RNA at that time. The Maoists' attack on a police check-post in Dunai on 25 September 2000, three-and-a-half years after their demand list was submitted, was a very significant event in the study of insurgency in Nepal and the relations between the government and the army.

Dunai is the headquarters of Dolpa district in the midwestern hills situated north of Rukum, one of the districts most affected by insurgency. The chief district officer of Dolpa had warned the Home Ministry in Kathmandu that the Maoists were planning an attack and had asked for reinforcements. As a result, forty-eight extra policemen were

---

6. Hutt, Michael (ed), *Nepal in the Nineties*, Oxford University Press, 1993.

7. Thapa and Sijapati, *A Kingdom under Siege*, The Printhouse, Kathmandu, 2003.

brought by helicopter to Dunai, the day before the attack. The Maoists attacked the next day with 1,000 guerrillas. Fighting continued for six hours and resulted in fourteen policemen dead, forty-one wounded and twelve missing. The Maoists also looted rupees fifty million in cash and jewellery from Nepal Bank. Rupees thirty-five million had been brought to the bank the previous day from Nepal Rastra Bank. It was not known why such a large amount had been brought into a district that had few development projects. Both the regional and zonal police chiefs were absent from the district at the time of the attack. It appeared as though the Maoists were aware of the money being transferred because they had delayed their attack. There was an RNA barracks in Dunai, a forty-minute walk from the site of attack.[8] The Maoist attack in Dunai led to the resignation of the Home minister who was from the Nepali Congress. Girija Koirala's government had wanted to mobilise the army in April 2001. According to the Constitution, such mobilisation could only be done by the king on the recommendation of the National Security Council. However, the recommendation was not implemented by King Birendra.[9]

After the massacre of the Royal family in June 2001, a committee was formed to investigate what had happened. As part of the proceedings, the committee interviewed Prajwal Shamsher Rana, commander-in-chief. He is reported to have said that the security of the Royal palace was not the responsibility of the RNA. He said the palace security was looked after by the military police, the ADC (aide de camp)

8. *Nepali Times*, 27 September '00.
9. *Deshantar*, 13 April '01.

and principal military secretary. However, he added that many military personnel inside the palace were sent on deputation from RNA.[10] Rana was appointed Royal Nepalese ambassador to France three years later after his retirement as COAS.

There were two rounds of peace talks between the government and the Maoists in August-September 2001. The Maoist agenda included repeal of the Armed Police Force Act. They said the RNA 'that is terrorising the people on various pretexts should be sent back to the barracks'.[11]

Prime Minister Girija Koirala wanted to deploy the RNA in insurgency-affected Rolpa in 2002. However, the top echelon of the RNA had decided that a pre-condition for deployment of the RNA would be an all-party consensus, imposition of a state of emergency and an anti-terrorism law.[12] Girija Koirala, in an interview to BBC in 2005, said the king turned down his request to use the military against the Maoists at a time when they had influence in only two places in the country.[13] Koirala resigned when this happened, and was replaced by Sher Bahadur Deuba. All of the above conditions were met before the RNA was mobilised. Some analysts have written that the army's reluctance to be used initially was due to the need for a legal basis for their actions and also so they could have complete charge of the situation, including controlling the press.[14] During Government-Maoist

10. *Kantipur*, 16 June '01.
11. *Kantipur*, 15 September '01.
12. Dhruba Kumar, 'The Royal Nepal Army', *Himal Southasia*, March-April 2006.
13. Mehta, Ashok, ibid.
14. Thapa and Sijapati, ibid.

talks in 2003, it was reportedly decided that the RNA would confine its activities to five kilometres around the barracks. However, the RNA and the Palace reportedly disagreed with this suggestion and it was not approved.[15]

COAS Prajwal Shamsher Rana addressed a convocation ceremony for command and staff training organised by RNA in April 2003 and commented on the situation in the country. He said a lack of good governance was responsible for the situation. While some people were blaming the RNA for the emergency that was imposed, he said it was really due to the political scenario existing for the last twelve years. There were demands that action be taken against Rana, after this speech. The argument was that he was an employee of the government, and should not have involved himself in politics. Prime Minister Deuba said it would be improper to confront a COAS at a time when the army was being used to attack insurgents. However, he did say that the COAS had been reprimanded.[16]

The 2003 Government-Maoist talks were termed a failure by the Maoists. Maoist leader Badal said, 'American imperialism has taken RNA, the principal power of the state, in its hands. RNA is responsible to the Americans and not to the nation.' He stated that even the king did not have control over the RNA.[17]

The Maoists attacked an RNA camp in Pilli in Kalikot district in the mid-western hills of Kalikot in Karnali in

15. Pandey, Nischal Nath, *Nepal's Maoist Movement and implications for India and China.*
16. Bijaya Kumar, 'Tito Satya', *Nepal,* 13 April '03.
17. Mahara, Krishna Bahadur, *Janadesh,* 7 June '03.

August 2005, killing forty-three soldiers. Deepak Gurung, spokesman of the RNA, blamed the INSAS rifles provided by India, which apparently failed to work properly, for the setback.[18]

India refuted this claim and said such weapons were being used by a million Indian army personnel, including Indian Para Military Forces, and added, 'Overall success in a war doesn't depend solely on weapons.'[19]

Maoist leader Prachanda had said in an interview granted to Indian daily *The Hindu* in Feburary 2006, that the Royal massacre would not have happened without the RNA. 'We are going towards a situation where RNA is in the driving seat', he added. He also accused the RNA for being loyal to the 'feudal lords' for more than two centuries. He asked 'democratic elements' in the RNA to join the SPA-Maoists. If elections were to take place, he said, international supervision over the RNA would be required.[20] Maoist leader Babu Ram Bhattarai proposed the 'Restructuring of both the RNA and PLA [People's Liberation Army] and the creation of a new national army according to the result of the Constituent Assembly elections'.[21] Maoist Supreme Leader Prachanda announced on 13 April that the SPA and Maoists had agreed to form a Democratic National Army after the RNA and PLA were organised.[22]

---

18. *Sanghu Weekly*, 15 August '05.
19. *The Kathmandu Post*, 19 August '05.
20. *The Hindu*, 9 February '06.
21. Bhattarai, Babu Ram, 'On Moriarty's Pontification', *The Kathmandu Post*, 23 February '06.
22. *Nepal Samacharpatra*, 13 April '06.

Concern about Human Rights Violations by RNA

There have been concerns expressed by human rights activists about violations by RNA in the conflict. There is now a human rights cell in RNA and the office of the UNHCR in Kathmandu. The Americans have taken credit for the establishment of a human rights cell as well as training provided to the military and civil police.[23] The director of UNHCR, Kathmandu Ian Martin has expressed concern about the use of helicopters by RNA in the conflict and the dropping of mortar bombs, which have been developed by the RNA. In one such incident, bombs were dropped in a school building in Thokarpa in Sindhupalchowk district adjoining Kathmandu valley, where the Maoists were holding a meeting. As it is difficult to distinguish between combatants and civilians in such an attack, they invited criticism.[24]

Ethnic Composition of RNA

No statistics are available on the ethnic composition of RNA. However, the percentage of Chhetris and Thakuris is supposed to be higher than British Gurkha or Indian Gurkha armies, which include a higher proportion of Janjatis, comprising Magars, Gurungs, Rais and Limbus. The Maoist army is also said to contain a large number of Magars: Maoist commanders as Ram Bahadur Thapa 'Badal', Barsaman Pun 'Ananta' and

---

23. Statement by Donald Camp, American deputy assistant secretary of state at Heritage Foundation, 3 March '03.
24. Hilton, Isabel, 'In Cahoots with the King', *The Guardian*, 11 April '06.

Nanda Kishor Pun 'Pasang' are all Magars. According to the 2001 census, more than half of the Magar community speaks Nepali as their mother tongue, and more than ninety percent follow Hinduism. Although both British and Indian Gurkha soldiers were listed as Hindus, most Gurungs listed their religion as Buddhism and many Rais and Limbus stated that they followed a religion called Kirat in the national census. However, the army celebrates Hindu festivals like Dashain regularly. The worship of Goddess Durga is undertaken by the RNA both during Bada Dashain in October and Chaite Dashain in the month of April in which goats and buffaloes are sacrificed.[25]

Shree Kali Bahadur Battalion consisting entirely of Gurungs and Shree Gorakh Nath Battalion, a mixed outfit, are stationed permanently as palace guards. On the other hand, Shree Singha Nath Battalion was converted as Rangers Battalion. Shri Bhairab Nath Battalion is a Special Forces battalion.[26]

All COAS of RNA since unification in 1768 have been Kshetriyas or Chheris or Thakuris. During the Rana regime (1846–1951) all were Ranas. Several non-Rana Chhetris such as Basnyat Thapa have also held the post since 1965.[27] However, there has never been a Magar, Gurung, Rai, Limbu or Brahmin COAS in spite of a substantial number of soldiers from these ethnic groups in RNA. Some writers have

25. Karki, Sushil Raj, Shahi Nepali Sena ra Dharmik Pakshya, Sipahi, BS 2049.
26. Mehta, ibid.
27. Khatri, Shiva Ram, Nepal Army Chiefs, Sira Khatri, Kathmandu, 1999.

commented on the 'monopoly' of Shah, Rana and Thapa clans in the senior posts in RNA. There were only thirteen out of fifty-three senior officers of RNA in 2004 who were Janjatis.[28]

Is a Military Coup in Nepal Possible?

In a book written in 1975 when the monarch was King Mahendra, scholar diplomat Rishikesh Shaha wrote that there was a personal bond between the king and the RNA and it regarded him as the sole personification of the state. He added that the RNA lacked the leadership to run the government of the country and a military coup was unlikely.[29] Could things have changed over the last three decades?

One Nepali writer has discussed such a possibility. If something unforeseen were to happen and Crown Prince Paras were to succeed, would he be able to protect Kathmandu from the Maoists? The writer suggests that the Americans might want to strengthen RNA or a group within RNA to prevent such a possibility.[30]

Ashok Mehta has written about the adverse impact of the suspension of Indian military aid to Nepal. He feels it could reduce the Indian Army's leverage over RNA and dilute traditional relations between the two armies. This could result in a lessening of Indian influence in Nepal.[31] In such a case,

28. Mehta, ibid.
29. Shaha, Rishikesh, Nepali Politics — Retrospect and Prospect.
30. Thapa, Manushree, 'The Recoup Scenario', *The Kathmandu Post*, 4 April '06.
31. Mehta, ibid.

Nepal might turn to China and Pakistan for arms supplies. Loosening of traditional ties between the two armies and lessening of Indian influence might prove disastrous for India in case there is a military coup in Nepal. Mehta says, 'A pro-India-rather than a pro-China or pro-Pakistan RNA is in the long-term interests of India'.[32] Mathew Kahane, resident representative of the United Nations Development Programme (UNDP) in Kathmandu, has said that if a government comprising political parties falls, then a takeover of an authoritarian nature by the army introducing martial law, emergency rule and suspension of human rights would be the worst-case scenario in Nepal.[33] What is interesting to note is that he has not ruled out the possibility of an army takeover in Nepal.

The Maoists have urged the formation of a 'Nepal National Army' — an integration of the RNA and the Maoist Army — after elections for a Constituent Assembly. There is likely to be a disagreement among officers in the RNA if and when such a scenario becomes a reality. As Maoist Supreme Leader Prachanda has stated in an interview recently, 'We can include lower ranks of RNA in our army. We have been saying to people of SPA, that you can become commander or commissar after joining PLA. Rank and File of RNA, Armed Police and Police is not our problem. It is only about 32 or so Generals that are our problem. If this could be ensured by peaceful and armed rebellion, their service could be continued. If we [the Maoists and SPA] could guarantee that their life and

---

32. Mehta, ibid.
33. *The Kathmandu Post*, 3 February '06.

employment will be ensured, the problem will be solved'.[34] The well-armed RNA having 100,000 troops might stage a military coup if that were to happen.

---

34. Interview with Prachanda, *Weekly Samaya*, 19 April '06.

6

Constituent Assembly:
Will it Solve the Maoist Problem?

The Maoists have been consistent in their demand for elections for a Constituent Assembly in Nepal. After the Twelve-Point Accord, major political parties including Nepali Congress and the CPN-UML, have also joined the Maoists in calling for a new Constitution.

Although the 1990 Constitution is not fully functional presently, it will become so as soon as elections for Parliament take place. There are several institutions in the country that still exist by virtue of the Constitution, including the Supreme Court and other Constitutional bodies such as the Public Service Commission and the Commission for Investigation for Abuse of Authority. Such provisions of the Constitution as fundamental rights have not been suspended. They were suspended briefly only during emergency. As formulating a new Constitution could be a time-consuming process, this may not be the best option in present-day Nepal.[1]

The Lower House of Parliament was dissolved on the recommendation of Prime Minister Deuba according to the Constitution. As he did not hold elections even six months after the dissolution, as required by the Constitution, he was dismissed by the king. Political parties demanded the resurrection of the dissolved Parliament, but this was denied by the Supreme Court. The last Parliament elected in 1999 would have continued for five years — till 2004 — had it not been dissolved. It is ridiculous on the part of the major political parties to continue to ask for its resurrection, even though its five-year period has already expired. It is even more ridiculous to ask for elections to a Constituent Assembly without getting rid of the present Constitution legally and according to due process. The only body that could ask for elections to a Constituent Assembly is a new Parliament elected by the sovereign people of Nepal, which can also amend the Constitution. The Speaker of the House of Representatives continues to hold his office even in 2006 as his tenure will end only when elections are held and a new Parliament is convened.

The 1990 Constitution contains certain features such as constitutional monarchy and multi-party system of democracy that cannot be amended. Although there is no provision for a referendum, an agreement could perhaps be made for such aspects in the future. It is important to remember in this context that the only referendum held in the history of Nepal

1. Interview with Surya Prasad Subedi, *Samaya*, November '05.

was in 1980 to decide whether the people wanted to continue the Panchayat system with appropriate reforms or a multi-party system. The Panchayat system won narrowly. Asking for restoration of a dissolved House would be similar to some degree as asking that the verdict of the 1980 referendum be respected in 2006.

If elections for a Constituent Assembly were to be called, the question remains as to who shall call it. It is only the sovereign people of Nepal who can call for such elections. As the monarch is bound by the 1990 Constitution, he cannot call for such elections. To agree that he could do so, would be to accept that it is the monarch and not the people of Nepal who have sovereign powers. The issue about the legal status of the Maoists and SPA that would entitle them to call elections to the Constituent Assembly remains in question as they are not sovereign bodies.[2]

India and the US, the two largest democracies in the world, had their Constitutions drafted by a Constituent Assembly. However, there is Maoist insurgency similar to Nepal in several states of India such as Jharkhand, Andhra Pradesh, Chhattisgarh, Orissa and Bihar. Not only is there democracy in India, but also in the states where the Maoist insurgency exists. Having a Constitution drafted by a Constituent Assembly did not prevent insurgency in India. Women in the US did not have the right to vote in the original Constitution but got that franchise in the early twentieth century by an amendment. Blacks got the right to vote in all of the states only after the Civil War. However, this could be

---

2. Raj, Prakash A., on Prachanda's Interviews, *The Kathmandu Post*, 24 February '06.

assured only in the 1960s. On the other hand, Nepal has given universal adult franchise to all its people. Even in Great Britain, the mother of all democracies, franchise was given to women only in the beginning of the twentieth century, several centuries after the signing of the *Magna Carta*.

The most important question before any elections are held, either for Parliament or for Constituent Assembly, is the question of arms held by the Maoists. What will happen to these *during*, and *after*, elections? As Keith George Bloomfield, the British ambassador to Nepal, has stated, 'The Maoists also need to demonstrate, in a far more convincing way than they have hitherto, that they recognize that their arms have to be put permanently beyond use if a political settlement is to be achieved. Without such a demonstration nobody in the country or in the international community will give their claimed conversion to democracy any credibility whatsoever.'

7

An Inclusive Agenda

One of the achievements of multi-party democracy in post-1990 Nepal was the end of censorship. The unprecedented freedom of expression led to a discussion of many issues that had not been allowed previously. Some people might say that such discussion would prove to be the remedy for the backwardness and discrimination that some groups were facing. On the other hand, others might feel that such discussions planted the seeds for the disintegration of Nepal.

Several ethnic activists in Nepal have protested against the disproportionate dominance of certain ethnic groups in the country, such as Chhetris, Bahuns and Thakuris, which make up only a third of the population of Nepal. Bahuns (a Nepali word for Brahmins) were found to be a dominant group not only in the Nepali Congress and CPN (UML),

People from Thimi Bhaktapur marching towards restricted area of Kathmandu, 15 April 2006.

Women demonstrators being arrested for agitating against the Royal government, 6 April 2006.

Two-wheelers struggling for petrol in front of Singh Durbar when curfew was lifted, 17 April 2006.

Photo-journalists busy collecting news and their footwear after an agitation, 23 April 2006.

A hundred thousand demonstrators gathered in front of Government Headquarters, Singh Durbar raise their arms in a spirit of victory, 9 April 2006.

A victory rally displaying placards with slogans on 25 April 2006.

Nepali youth demonstrating even though hurt, during rallies at Patan on 7 April 2006.

UML, Ramkumari Jhankri leading the mass rally inside the Patan core area on 7 April 2006.

Youth of seventh-party participating in a demonstration against the Royal government, 6 April 2006.

Women from Patan Gahabal participating in a demonstration with their domestic implements, 4 April 2006.

In Jhochhen, ladies of Seventh-party arrested for entering the restricted area, 7 April 2006.

At Mandala Park, paying condolences to 1,269 people killed during 2062 (bikram sambet) year by lighting candles, 14 April 2006.

Senior members of the society in discussion at the TUIOM to put pressure on the government to withdraw curfew imposed, 8 April 2006, Maharajgunj.

Senior members of society leading the mass rally during the curfew, 8 April 2006, Maharajgunj.

Police making arrests during a peace demonstration, 8 April 2006, Maharajgunj.

Arrested persons in the police van. From left, Padma Ratna Tuladhar, Malla K. Sundar, Dr Madhu Ghimire, Shanta Dixit and former speaker Daman Nath Dhungana, 8 April 2006.

Seven-parties holding a torch rally at Keltole Massangalli against the Royal government, March 2006.

Party activists gather at "Sahid Manch" open air theater, 15 April 2006.

Government staff participating in a victory rally, Baneshwar, 25 April 2006.

Burning the photos of members of the Royal family at Bagbazar, 6 April 2006.

Masses gather in front of the open air theater to listen to speeches and wave flags of the NC and UML, 9 April 2006.

Armed policemen march towards demonstrators to disperse the rally at Kalanki, 8 April 2006.

The armed policemen running for cover to escape tear gas bombs thrown at them by the activists, 23 April 2006.

MPV entering the core area of the main bazaar, New Road, 6 April 2006.

but also among the Maoists. If Girija Koirala and Krishna Prasad Bhattarai were Brahmin Nepali Congress leaders who were made prime ministers, Manmohan Adhikari, the first Communist prime minister of Nepal from CPN (UML), was also a Bahun. Leaders from the UML, such as Madhav Kumar Nepal, Bam Dev Gautam and Bharat Mohan Adhikari, who were deputy prime ministers, were also Bahuns. Three other prime ministers post-1990 — Surya Bahadur Thapa, Lokendra Bahadur Chand and Sher Bahadur Deuba — were all Chhetris or Thakuris, also called Kshetriyas.

There have only been three prime ministers after the unification of Nepal in 1768, who were not from these communities: Sarbajit Rana Magar, during the regency of Rajendralaxmi, daughter-in-law of King Prithvi Narayan Shah, Ranga Nath Paudel, a Bahun, during the regency of Samrajyalaxmi before the advent of the Rana regime in 1830s, and Marichman Singh, a Newar, during the concluding days of the Panchayat era in 1990.

The two top leaders of the Maoists, Prachanda and Baburam Bhattarai, are both Bahuns. Bahuns also predominate the civil services. There were many Sanskrit medium schools in Nepal where admission was restricted mostly to Bahuns. As the Nepali language, especially in the written form is saturated with Sanskrit, knowledge of this language gave Bahuns an advantage while competing in the civil service exams. Most judges and employees in judicial service are also Bahuns. On the other hand, Chhetris predominate the RNA.

Bahuns, Chhetris and Thakuris are high caste Hindus whose first language is Nepali. There has been a feeling of alienation on the part of many groups such as Janjatis, Dalits and Madhises living in the Terai who speak such languages as Maithili, Bhojpuri and Awadhi. On the other hand, Newars have the highest per capita income in the country and are concentrated not only in Kathmandu valley, which was their original habitat, but also towns all along Nepal where they migrated after unification in search of commercial opportunities. They were represented in the civil services, disproportionately to their percentage in population (which was 5.5). As they lived in the capital and district headquarters they were comparatively affluent and literate. They were also classified as Janjatis. They claimed that they were exploited by dominant classes (Bahun, Chhetri, Thakuri) although there are more Hindus among Newars than Buddhists.[1] Some non-Hindus objected to Nepal being called a Hindu kingdom although the Hindus made up more than eighty percent of the population in 2001, a decline of six percent since the previous census in 1991. Many people in several ethnic groups that were previously classified as Hindus, such as Rais and Limbus, claimed that they were following the Kirat religion and were not Hindus. On the other hand, some ethnic activists such as Dr Harka Gurung and Krishna Bhattachan advised the ethnic communities to write their religion as Buddhist instead of Hindu and their mother tongue as their original language and not Nepali, irrespective of whatever religion they were following or language they were speaking. To some extent, this could be attributed to *search for,* and *assertion of,*

---

1.   Sharma, Prayag Raj, 'Nation-Building, Multi-Ethnicity, and the Hindu State', in Gellner, Pfaff-Czarnecka and Whelpton, *Nationalism and Ethnicity in a Hindu Kingdom,* Harwood Academic Publishers, Amsterdam, 1997.

identity. More than half of Magars and about a third of Newars had adopted Nepali as their mother tongue. Advice given to falsify census data was unbecoming of scholars.

Dalits form 13.8 percent of the population of Nepal, according to the 2001 census. These are classified as hill Dalits speaking Nepali as their mother tongue and Terai Dalits speaking such languages as Maithili, Bhojpuri and Awadhi. Hill Dalits form about eight percent of the population. Three general elections were held in Nepal after restoration of multi-party democracy and under the 1990 Constitution. It was reported[2] that only one Dalit could be elected to the House of Representatives in these elections. However, eight Dalits were nominated to the Rashtriya Sabha or the Upper House post 1990. Ramprit Paswan was elected vice-chairman of the Rashtriya Sabha.

Although the 1990 Constitution requires that five percent of nominees of political parties for Parliament must be women, no Dalit women were nominated. Dalits in India are given reservations of a certain number of seats in Parliament. They are also given reservation in certain number of posts in the civil services. No such provision exists in Nepal. Countries like the United States have adopted affirmative action to the minorities. Some kind of reservations or affirmative action should be given to Dalits in Nepal.[3]

---

2. Raj, Prakash A., 'Dalit Mahila ko Rajnaitik Adhikar' in Jha, Haribansh (ed), Terai ka Dalit ebam Dalit Mahila, Centre for Economic and Technical Studies, Kathmandu, 2003.
3. Ibid.

Nepal is recognised as a multi-ethnic and multi-lingual country according to the 1990 Constitution. However, it is not called a multi-religious country. Kanak Dixit, editor of the magazine *Himal*, has said that the definition of Nepal as a Hindu country, 'Can be considered a human rights abuse of those who are Buddhists, Moslem, Christian, nature worshippers, non-religious and so on'.[4] This is a ridiculous argument, as non-Hindus in Nepal have full freedom to practice their religion.

The word 'inclusive' is often used in present-day Nepal, to stress the fact that many groups such as Janjatis, Dalits, Madhesis and women have yet to become part of mainstream society. The Maoists have put this on their agenda. This represents only part of the truth and not the whole truth. The Nepal Federation of Nationalities has classified some groups as indigenous Adibasi, which had entered Nepal from Tibet five centuries earlier. These include the Sherpas. On the other hand, Khas (Chhetris) living in mid-western and far-western hills have not been classified as Adibasis. There is a trend to use the terms Adibasi and Janjati as synonyms, which is not correct. Many Janjatis have adopted Nepali as their mother-tongue and profess Hinduism. The caretakers (*pujaris*) in many Hindu temples in Nepal are Janjatis such as these. There has been a trend among tribes in Nepal to adopt Hinduism and the Nepali language.

The most backward area in Nepal consists of the hilly region in mid-west and far-west situated between Bheri river in the east to Mahakali river in the west. A study conducted

4. Dixit, Kanak, 'Till Kingdom Come', *The Times of India*, 14 November '97.

by Dutch development agency SNV and ICIMOD (Integrated Center for Mountain Development) found that the most backward districts in Nepal in terms of low per capita income, literacy, poverty and deprivation were these districts. An analysis of ethnic composition of the area demonstrates that more than half of the population consisted of high caste Hindus (Bahuns, Chhetris and Thakuris).[5]

Nepali language in Nepal is a link language and has been granted the status of *Rashtra Bhasa*, national language, under the 1990 Constitution. The Constitution also gives it the status of the sole official language of the country: the language in which the government will conduct its business. On the other hand, other languages spoken in Nepal are called *Rashtriya Bhasa*, technically meaning non-official national languages.

Municipalities in Kathmandu Metropolis, Mahanagar-palika, granted the status of official language to Newari sometime in mid-1990s. Similarly, the District Development Committee at Saptari granted the status of second official language to Maithili. A writ petition was filed in the Supreme Court to invalidate the status given to these languages. The Supreme Court ruled that the order granting second official language status to Newari and Maithili was unconstitutional as only Nepali was granted such status according to the 1990 Constitution.

Nepal would need to follow an inclusive agenda in the future. There is now a consensus that such an agenda should be made either by amending the 1990 Constitution or by drafting a new Constitution by the Constituent Assembly.

---

5. Raj, Prakash A., Bahujatiya Bahubhasiya Nepal, Nabeen Publications, *Kathmandu*, BS 2056.

This should be done to alleviate the feeling of alienation and to ensure that backward regions and communities are made part of mainstream society. Whether this can be done by introducing reservation in Parliament or by requiring political parties to give a certain percentage of seats to the disadvantaged or by affirmative action should be debated in Parliament. There are some who have advocated the creation of autonomous regions in the country based on ethnicity with its own legislature having proportional representation of linguistic, ethnic and ethnic groups.[6] It seems correct to assume that an inclusive peace process is essential in view of the history of exclusion in Nepal, as well as Nepal's identity as a multi-ethnic and multi-lingual country.[7]

---

6. Bhattachan, Krishnabahadur, Naya Rajyasamrachanako Prastab, *Kantipur*, 8 August '05.
7. Philipson, Liz, 'Negotiating Peace', *Himal Southasia*, March-April 2006.

8

India — the Closest Neighbour

Nepal's relations with India have become increasingly important since November 2005, after the signing of the Twelve-Point Accord between the Maoists and the Seven Party Alliance agitating for a restoration of multi-party democracy in Nepal.

A Historical Overview

King Prithvi Narayan Shah, who initiated Nepal's unification in 1768, called it a yam between two boulders, meaning India and China.

The relations between Nepal and British India were quite friendly after the signing of the Treaty of Sugauli in 1816. Nepal had assisted the British in quelling the First War of Independence in 1857, and in return received a part of western Terai, called 'Naya Muluk' consisting of present-day Banke, Bardia, Kailali and Kanchanpur districts, which it had lost in the Treaty of Sugauli. Nepal was recognised as a fully sovereign and independent country according to a Treaty signed between Nepal and the British in 1923, partly in appreciation of the help Nepal gave the Allies during the First World War. Had it not been for this Treaty, Nepal could have been absorbed in India in the same way as the Indian princely states of Hyderabad and Patiala.

When the British left India after Independence in 1947, a new equation emerged in relations between the two countries. India helped the anti-Rana forces overthrow the Ranas and bring democracy to the country. King Tribhuwan — who had been given asylum in India — returned to Nepal triumphantly, marking the advent of democracy in the country. Indo-Nepal relations, in the fifty-five years since then, have been characterised by periods of several ups and downs. During the early 1950s, India was the dominant power in Nepal and the relations remained close when B.P. Koirala was prime minister. His dismissal in December 1960 was termed a 'setback to democracy' by Prime Minister Nehru.

Nepali insurgents operating from India tried to overthrow the royal regime of King Mahendra in 1961-62; an operation which failed due to Sino-Indian border conflict in 1962. China saved the royal regime in Nepal at that time. Towards the end of the Panchayat regime in the late 1980s, the Indian blockade of Nepal, caused partly by Nepal's purchase of arms from China without the knowledge or consent of India, and the personal chemistry between King Birendra and Prime Minister Rajiv Gandhi, was one of the catalysts for the eventual overthrow of the Panchayat regime in April 1990, transfer of sovereignty to the people of Nepal and the enforcement of a multi-party system of government.

During the twelve years of multi-party democracy between 1990 and 2002, relations between the two countries remained friendly. Although India signed separate treaties of trade and transit with Nepal, it allowed Bhutanese refugees to enter the country via Indian territory and did not pressurise Bhutan to take them back. India remained concerned about threats to its security interests from activities of Islamic militants alleged to be supported by Pakistan's Inter Services Intellligence (ISI) from Nepalese territory. An Indian Airlines aircraft was hijacked from Kathmandu on Christmas eve in 1999, and landed in Kandahar in Taliban-ruled Afghanistan. There have been attacks by terrorists in India in the Indian Parliament, Akshardham Temple in Gujarat and Sankat Mochan Temple in Varanasi in recent years. It is possible that Nepalese territory might have been used in providing logistic support for such attacks.

There is more than 1,800 km of unregulated and open border between the two countries, as Nepal shares its borders with Sikkim, West Bengal, Bihar, Uttar Pradesh and Uttaranchal. Nepal should be sensitive to India's security concerns as its own security might be affected. Actually, the Indo-Nepal border along the 'heartland' of India is also India's soft underbelly, the de-stabilisation of which could seriously affect India's security. Nepal should go out of its way to assure India that its security will not be threatened from happenings in Nepal. A Nepali court has recently convicted four Kashmiris for supplying information and financial aid from Nepalese territory to Kashmir-based separatist group Hizbul Mujahadin.

Both India and China are, at present, booming economies characterised by high growth rates. Sino-Indian trade is limited at present, but has shown prospects for tremendous growth especially in western China. There are possibilities that Kodari Road and Rasuwa Road — currently being constructed for this purpose — will enable the use of Nepal as a transit point. This is primarily because the Nathu-La Pass in Sikkim is not suitable for year-round trade and the former Stilwel Road connecting Assam with Yunan via Myanmar (formerly Burma) is not operational. In fact, India had asked Nepal whether it could be used as a transit point. Nepal's India policy should be to encourage the development of the country as a transit point for Sino-Indian trade.

Indo-Nepal Relations since King Gyanendra's Takeover

Indo-Nepal relations in the three-and-a-half years since the dismissal of Sher Bahadur Deuba in October 2002 and after the royal takeover on 1 February 2005 have not been marked by cordiality. India has suspended military aid to Nepal, aid that is required to fight the insurgents. Although such persons as K. Natwar Singh and J.N. Dixit — who were powerful in the late 1980s and were mainly responsible for the deterioration in Indo-Nepal relations at that time and who both resumed positions of power when the UPA came to power — are now no longer on the scene, relations have not improved. Perhaps King Gyanendra's attitude towards India could have been more accommodating.

There are two schools of thought in India regarding the Royal takeover. While the South Block had initially been very critical and had suspended all military aid, it appeared that the Ministry of Defence and the Indian Army did not seem to be in favour of stopping all military aid to Nepal. Although India is a democratic country where the armed forces are under the control of the elected government, such difference of opinion seems somewhat surprising. Indian columnists have confirmed the divide between the Foreign Ministry and Defence Ministry in what is reported to be the 'most sweeping reassessment of India's Nepal policy since 1990'.[1] Quoting a South Block official in New Delhi, an influential Indian newspaper had reported: 'While a Maoist victory in Nepal is unlikely, India would not be fazed by such an eventuality'.[2]

A leading advocate of the first school of thought is Prof. S.D. Muni of Jawaharlal Nehru University in Delhi who has also taught the Maoist leader Baburam Bhattarai when he was a student in the 1980s. It has been his view that the Maoists in Nepal are not a threat to India and could even provide a 'moderating influence on the Naxalites in India if they were to come to power in Nepal'.[3] The Maoist supreme leader Prachanda, while replying to a question on the Naxalite movement in India, said a multi-party system in Nepal including the Maoists would send a signal to the Naxalites in India.[4] There are many in position of authority in the Indian establishment who support this theory. Satish Chandra, former deputy national security advisor to the Government

1. *The Hindu*, 14 May '05.
2. *The Hindustan Times*, 16 February '06.
3. Muni, S.D., *Maoist Insurgency in Nepal*, Rupa & Co, New Delhi, 2003.
4. *The Hindu*, 10 February '06.

of India, has written recently that a Maoist takeover in Nepal could take place within several months. He writes, '[If there is] a Maoist takeover at some point in time, then so be it. In such an eventuality we should be prepared to accept it as the lesser of two evils'. He believes military supplies to Nepal were suspended after the royal coup because it is in India's national interests to have done so.[5] An Indian columnist has written about a point of view in Delhi which states that: 'the inherent conservatism of the Indian security establishment prevents New Delhi from totally abandoning the King'.[6]

There are others who believe that Indian national interests demand that India should start dealing with King Gyanendra. As columnist Vikram Sood states in *The Hindustan Times*[7], the king is the only symbol of authority left and spurning him will not help the situation. He feels Nepal is a vital security risk for India, and its security interests need to be safeguarded. The Maoists in India are allied with those in Nepal and there is a 'revolutionary corridor' from Bihar on the Indo-Nepal border to the coastal areas in Andhra Pradesh. He also talks about Maoist leaders and cadres and affected refugees taking shelter in India. Stating that the Indian military has understood the common dangers facing both Nepal and India, senior Indian journalist Swapan Das Gupta believes 'India's national and strategic interests have been mortgaged' by a few persons in South Block. He talks about the possibility of India needing to hold up a 'factitious and unreliable democratic

---

5. *The Hindu*, 10 February '05.
6. Varadarajan, Siddhartha, 'US and India Part Company on Nepal', *The Hindu*, 22 February '06.
7. 16 May '05.

regime' if monarchy were to be crippled and there was a possibility of direct Indian intervention in Nepal to control the Maoists.

India's former Ambassador to Nepal K.V. Rajan has stated, 'India, too, must accept its share of responsibility — it has been a passive spectator for far too long, despite the obvious dangers it poses to its own security. There is no excuse for the fact that despite frequent communications from the Nepalese side, Maoist leaders for the past few years have been moving freely across the border, holding meetings with senior Nepalese politicians on Indian soil, without Indian agencies apparently knowing about it.'[8]

What then are India's national interests that could be threatened if Nepal were to be ruled by a regime that is insensitive to India's security interests? Nepal is situated just north of India's 'heartland', consisting of eastern Uttar Pradesh and northern Bihar. The area is agrarian, and economically backward, and is made up of almost a fourth of India's population. The Indo-Nepal border is an open one: neither a passport nor any other identity papers are required to cross it. Although India has now started to implement a project under which some kind of identity papers will be required along certain sectors to cross the border, it still remains unguarded and open. There is Naxalite activity stretching from Bihar, Jharkhand, Chhattisgarh, Orissa and Andhra Pradesh by groups that are members of the RIM, similar to Nepalese Maoists. This is called the 'Red Corridor',

---

8. Rajan, K.V., 'Nepal', in Dixit, J.N. (ed), *External Affairs: Cross-Border Relations*, Roli Books, New Delhi, 2003.

and includes a stretch from north Telangana in Andhra Pradesh to Chhattisgarh, which is called 'liberated zone'.[9]

There is only a twenty-kilometre wide Indian territory at 'Chicken's Neck' between Nepal and Bangladesh. There are more than 100,000 Bhutanese refugees of Nepalese origin in the camps there. There are also extremist organisations such as Khumbuwan Liberation Front in the hills north of Jhapa. The Maoists in Nepal have already declared the hilly area in eastern Nepal as Kirat Autonomous Region. If forces inimical to Indian interests were to capture power there, India's hold on the entire northeast, consisting of such states as Assam, Meghalaya, Nagaland, Manipur, Mizoram and Arunachal Pradesh, could be threatened. A news report published in *The Times of India* said that Uttaranchal could become a 'catchment region for Maoists' as some bordering districts of Pithoragarh, Champawat and Udham Singh Nagar were already forming a 'gateway for men and arms from Maoist strongholds in Nepal'. If armed activity were to gain root, it would be virtually impossible to control.[10]

Four districts in south-western Nepal — Banke, Bardia, Kailali and Kanchanpur — are geographically closer to New Delhi than to Kathmandu; the city of Mahendranagar in Kanchapur district is only a four hours' drive from New Delhi. All of the above four districts are under the control of the Maoists, excluding the district headquarters. The Rohilkhand Division in western Uttar Pradesh, situated between New

---

9. Sinha, Rakesh, 'Revolution meets Confusion', *The Indian Express*, 16 November '05.

10. Ghildiyal, Subodh, 'Next Stop for Red Terror: Uttaranchal', *The Times of India*, 17 April '06.

Delhi and Kanchanpur and including such districts as Moradabad, Bareilly and Rampur, also has a large percentage of Muslims. These are some of the factors that affect Indian national interests and the Indian policy regarding the Nepalese Maoist insurgents.

A seminar on 'Restoring Peace and Stability in Nepal' was held on 6-7 December 2004 in New Delhi. It was organised by the India International Centre but indirectly sponsored by the Indian Foreign Ministry. One of the interesting aspects of the seminar was the presentation of scenarios by the Institute of Defence Studies and analysis by a retired general of the Indian Army. The participants were presented four scenarios. Under the first scenario, an attempt on the life of the monarch is made but he escapes unhurt and the situation worsens as strikes and ISI-sponsored activities increase. There are demands by the king for intervention from India. The second scenario is that the Maoists keep in touch with China and declare a 'People's Republic' in Nepal and ISI supplies arms to the Maoists. China mobilises an army to the border. The king asks for Indian intervention. The third scenario finds the political parties increasing contact with the Maoists and the role of the RNA increases. There is increasing contact between the Maoists in Nepal and Naxalite outfits in India. The fourth scenario finds a deteriorating situation and the king considers going into exile. The Maoists declare a 'People's Republic', and there is the possibility that the US might increase military support, Pakistan's ISI could supply arms to the Maoists and possible intervention by China. The king asks for military assistance from the US and China. China warns both the US and India against intervening in Nepal.

It appeared that India was not in favour of a joint intervention against the Maoists but would welcome co-ordinated operation as had happened against the ULFA insurgents in Bhutan. It was surprising why such an analysis was shown to participants in a seminar that included two former foreign ministers of Nepal, a former speaker of Parliament, a former Maoist, an editor of a monthly allegedly close to the Maoists, a retired major general of RNA, and three journalists.

Nepal has not been able to take advantage of the goodwill of the Indian armed forces and India has its policy formed solely by South Block and the intelligence agencies. It is time to ask if Indian security concerns in Nepal have been addressed. Indo-Nepalese relations at present seem to be characterised by misunderstanding and a lack of appreciation of each others' concerns.

As the popular movement against the monarchy gathered momentum by mid-April 2006, there were also concerns in India about what would happen in Nepal. The Naxalites in India were also increasing their activities, especially in Chhattisgarh, Andhra Pradesh and Jharkhand. India's decision to send a special envoy and its foreign secretary to Nepal was a very important one as it was taking place at a crucial time and also because the diplomats were to convey the Indian government's concerns about Nepal to its monarch.

9

China — the Northern Neighbour

The Chinese government has been opposed to the Maoists borrowing the name of their great leader Mao. They call them 'anti-government forces' instead. The Chinese president, Hu Jintao, had condemned terrorist activity in Nepal and offered moral support in crushing the insurgency during King Gyanendra's visit to China in July 2002. Chinese Ambassador Wu Congyong, at a programme in June 2002, stated that China would provide necessary assistance to Nepal to establish peace in the country. However, the Chinese did not call the insurgents terrorists. The Maoist leaders have said complimentary things about the Chinese in their articles, even naming their party after the Chinese leader and their army as PLA (People's Liberation Army). Baburam Bhattarai has written that the Americans were trying to encircle China. However, the Chinese have not reciprocated the complimentary things the Maoists in Nepal had to say about China.[1]

The visit of Chinese State Counsellor Tang Jiaxuan, the first such visit since the royal takeover on 1 February 2005 by the highest-ranking Chinese official was eagerly awaited in Nepal. There was a great deal of interest in how the Chinese are viewing the Maoist insurgency in Nepal and how they would react if the current situation were to change. It could definitely be said that his statements on the situation in Nepal had the approval from the highest echelons of power in Beijing. Let us analyse what he did say, what he did not say and what the implications are. Is there any change in the traditional Chinese stand on Nepal? His statements are especially important in the context of the Twelve-Point Accord between the Seven Party Alliance and the Maoists and the recent meeting between the two sides held in Delhi.

Tang met King Gyanendra, vice chairman of the Council of Ministers and the foreign minister, which is usually the norm during official visits. What is important is that he also met the leaders of political parties: the first ever such step by a visiting Chinese leader in Kathmandu. The leaders included Girija Prasad Koirala of Nepali Congress, Bharat Mohan Adhikari and Amrit Kumar Bohara of UML and Nepali Congress (Democratic) leader Sher Bahadur Deuba. China has reiterated its previous stand that there should be no interference in Nepal's internal affairs by any 'outside forces'. He has also stated 'constitutional forces will seek to appropriately settle the current difficulties through dialogue,

---

1. Raj, Prakash A., Maoist Insurgency in Chinese Eyes, *The Himalayan*, 31 May '03.

based on the maintenance of Nepal's independence, sovereignty and national unification'. The term 'constitutional forces' means the monarch and the political parties. As the Maoists do not support the present Constitution and are calling for elections for a Constitutional Assembly, they are not constitutional forces as Tang's statement would seem to imply.

The United States has also been advocating that the king reach out to the political parties and for restoration of democratic institutions as the American President said at a press conference during his visit to India. He also asked the Maoists to renounce violence. However, the Chinese state counsellor did not even as much as mention anything about the Maoists during his trip to Nepal. Of course, the Chinese do call the Maoists 'anti-government forces'. Tang did not mention the accord between the Maoists and the Seven Party Alliance that was signed in Delhi. Since the Maoists are asking for elections to the Constituent Assembly and the Seven Party Alliance have also joined the Maoists in asking for a Constituent Assembly along with the Chinese asking for a dialogue between 'constitutional forces', this leaves the Maoists out and could be said to imply a disapproval of the accord. In an interview given to The Hindu,[2] a daily published from India, Prachanda has said that the Chinese were worried about the situation inside Nepal and believed that it needed a careful resolution. According to him, they had always said that the matter was Nepal's internal problem. Prachanda believes China and India need to work together in favour of democracy and people of Nepal. This appears to be mere

---

2. 10 February '06.

wishful thinking on the part of the Maoist leader. What is important to remember is that Chinese and Indian national interests do not necessarily coincide regarding their policy on Nepal. If they had identical interests, the Chinese would not have warned India not to interfere in Nepal in 1961. Just because the Chinese said they were worried about the situation in Nepal and met the leaders of political parties in Nepal, it does not necessarily imply that they would follow an identical policy regarding Nepal.

The Chinese have never interfered in Nepal's internal affairs. No insurgents against Nepal have operated from Chinese territory nor have they received asylum there. They are interested in stability in their neighbourhood as they are involved in the task of development in the western part of the country including Tibet and Sinkiang. India has asked Nepal to be a transit point for trade with China. This is primarily because both India and China are booming economies with a high growth rate. As the road linking Tibet via Nathu La in Sikkim lacks the necessary infrastructure and is not open all year around, and Stilwel Road built during the Second World War connecting Yunan and Assam is not yet open all along its length presently, Nepal would be an ideal transit point for Sino-Indian trade. Such trade will be beneficial to all three countries. As far as China is concerned, such trade will help develop Tibet. Unrest in Nepal characterised by frequent strikes, 'Nepal Bandha' and 'blockade' will cripple the Nepalese economy and lead Nepal to becoming a 'failed state'. It will not be in China's interest if Nepal were to become a 'failed state' as it could invite external intervention in Nepal that could also affect Chinese control over Tibet. The Chinese are very sensitive on this issue as there are many external forces which want to threaten Chinese control over Tibet. The Chinese may also be concerned as the insurgency has spread to such districts bordering Tibet as Humla, Dolakaha and Sindhu Palchok that is traversed by Kodari Road, one of few roads linking Tibet with the subcontinent. There are many ethnic Tibetans living in these districts. The Maoist insurgents are using sophisticated weapons, which are supplied externally and could possibly have been purchased from an international arms market. China will be concerned if some of these might find their way inside Tibet.[3] There is now a strategic partnership between the US, India and China. The US now regards China as an economic and strategic rival. As there is already a road linking Tibet from Nepal and several more are planned including that passing through Rasuwa, Nepal's strategic importance will increase.

Counsellor Tang's meeting with leaders of political parties signifies Chinese endorsement of dialogue and conciliation between the king and the political parties. It is interesting to note that the view of both China and the US in asking for re-conciliation between the king and the political parties are similar. Both the palace and the political parties should heed the Chinese view in this matter. The US and one of Nepal's neighbours share identical views on this matter. Although India still pays lip service to its policy of being supportive of constitutional monarchy and multi-party democracy, there are some in Nepal who doubt India's motive in this matter. On the other hand, Tang has stated that 'China is ready to

3. Pandey, Nischal Nath, *Nepal's Maoist Movement and Implications for India and China*, Manohar, 2005.

increase friendly exchanges with the Nepalese royal family, government, political parties and people of all walks of life and expand bilateral exchanges and cooperation in politics, economy, trade, culture and tourism'. One of the important aspects of Tang's address deals with his emphasis on 'stability' in Nepal as well as in the region as a whole. He believes a stable Nepal promotes regional peace, stability and development. It could be implied that a stable Nepal will also promote stability in the entire region including Tibet Autonomous Region in China.

One interesting question is how China will react if external forces attempt to topple the current regime in Nepal. Would it be like in 1961 when the Chinese Foreign Minister Chen Yi gave his famous statement warning outside powers not to interfere in Nepal, which was to save Nepal? On the other hand, would the Chinese react as they did in 1989 when they were too preoccupied with internal matters and could not help Nepal during the Indian blockade? When this question was put to two former foreign ministers of Nepal one replied: 'The Chinese would not do anything except giving token support'. The other said: 'The Chinese will not hand over Nepal to any regional power read India on a platter this time. China was preoccupied with internal matters in 1989 and is less so now. The railway line connecting Lhasa with the mainland is almost complete. This will facilitate movement of goods, arms and even troops should need arise, to the border.' In view of the strategic importance of Nepal, the change that has taken place in Tibet in recent years, and the strategic alliance between India and the United States, it remains to be seen which of the two analysis is more trustworthy.[4] However, because of the huge amount of Sino-American trade in recent years, Chinese investment in American security and bond market and also the similar viewpoint between the Americans and the Indians with regard to Nepal, makes it less likely that the Chinese would provide more than a token support to Nepal even if India were to intervene.

4. Raj, Prakash A., *China's Nepal Policy*, *People's Review*, 6 April '06.

10

The Superpower and its Shadow

*If the Royal Nepalese Army (RNA) had not become Royal American
Army, we'd have captured Kathmandu two years earlier.*
— Maoist leader Prachanda,
(Interview to *Weekly*, Nepal, 21 April 2006)

The end of the Cold War and the disintegration of the
Soviet Union and the emergence of the United States
as the sole Superpower led to new relationships
between states in South Asia. The United States was to become
a strategic partner of India that had been an ally of the
erstwhile Soviet Union. China had emerged as a strategic
and economic rival of the United States by the beginning of
the new millennium. The terrorist attacks on the Twin Towers

in New York was a factor that led to increased interest in Asia including Nepal. This was written in 2004 with reference to American interest in Nepal: 'Had the world remained bi-polar with India allied with the Soviet Union, had there been no terrorist attack on the US on 9/11 resulting in India and the US finding common grounds to fight fundamentalism and terrorism, had Nepal not been facing an insurgency to establish a communist state, it is unlikely that US interest in Nepal would have manifested in the present form. Nepal's present situation created an impression among US policy makers that it might become a "failed state", which like Afghanistan may be a breeding ground for ultra terrorist groups endangering the security of the USA as well. This could have been a major factor in increasing American interest in Nepal in recent years'.[1] By 2006 American interest in Nepal had increased considerably and both the government and the Maoists regarded it as having utmost importance. Although the US had provided foreign aid to Nepal for more than fifty years from 1951 to 2000 amounting to $500 million, it had not regarded it as an important country. Spiro T. Agnew, the American vice president under Richard Nixon who was forced to resign some time later had visited Nepal in 1968 but it was more like a junket. The first ever visit by an American secretary of state took place in Nepal in 2002 when Colin Powell visited Nepal.

James F. Moriarty, the American ambassador to Nepal, has now become an important figure in Nepal in view of

---

1. Raj, Prakash A., Recent trends of US Interest in Nepal, *Nepal's Relations with United States of America*, Institute of Foreign Affairs, Kathmandu, 2004.

American policy towards the country including its stand on the Maoist insurgents. While he has reiterated that the American policy towards Nepal has not changed despite the change in the ambassador, he has also called the Maoists to lay down arms. He has also said that the US is in favour of mediation by the UN to bring about dialogue between the government of Nepal and the Maoists.

On the other hand, Ambassador Michael Malinowsky, his predecessor, had compared the Maoists to such terrorists as Khmer Rouge, Shining Path or Al Qaida after visiting the site of Maoist attack at Achham in western Nepal.[2] Does this represent a real change on how the US is viewing the insurgency? After the signing of the agreement between SPA and the Maoists in November 2005, Moriarty was asked about his reaction and whether he felt the Maoists were committed to joining the political mainstream. He replied that 'the Maoists pledge their partnership with the parties, until ... they don't need them any longer'. What would happen if the SPA and the Maoists were able to topple the monarchy? He felt the Maoists would be armed and the parties unarmed. The Maoists would have neutralised most or parts of the RNA, leaving the parties defenceless against the Maoists. He added that the Maoists took arms against a functioning parliamentary system when they took arms in 1996.[3] Baburam Bhattarai has stated that there was a nexus between 'the US imperialist ruling classes and Nepal's feudal autocratic forces' as Moriarty had appealed to the SPA to ignore their agreement

2. Malinowski, Michael, 'Maoists are same as Khmer Rouge or Al Qaida', *Spotlight*, 1 March '02.
3. *The Telegraph Weekly*, 22 January '06.

signed in November 2005 and reconcile with the king. He said the Maoists had committed to multi-party competitive politics in the future. He believed RNA was not a 'logical source of defence' for the parliamentary parties and democracy' but was used by monarchy to stage coup d'etats in 1960 and 2003-05'.[4]

President George Bush commented on US policy about Nepal during a press conference during his official trip to India in March 2006. He said, ' We agreed that the Maoists should abandon violence and the King should reach out to the political parties to restore democratic institutions.' Prime Minister Manmohan Singh was also present there and the word 'we' implied both India and the US. It is interesting to note that President Bush did not call the Maoists, terrorists. It appears that the Americans don't believe there is a military solution to the conflict and seem not to be in a hurry to resume lethal arms supply to Nepal.[5] Donald Camp, the deputy assistant secretary of state for South and Central Asian Affairs visited Nepal in March 2006. He said after his meeting with the king that the US wouldn't recognise parliamentary elections scheduled to be held in 2006 if they were held in the same manner as the municipal polls. However, he was not convinced about any 'breakthrough' in restoring democratic institutions in Nepal.[6]

---

4. Bhattarai, Baburam, 'On Moriarty's Pontification', *The Kathmandu Post*, 23 February '06.
5. Adhikary, Druba H, American Message from Delhi, *The Kathmandu Post*, 11 March '06.
6. *The Kathmandu Post*, 10 March '06.

The major objectives of the US policy in Nepal are restoration of multi-party democracy and preventing a Maoist takeover. It has been critical of the 1 February royal takeover and has also been critical of RNA when serious human rights abuses such as arbitrary detentions, disappearance of detainees and torture are reported. It had suggested that political parties should be brought to participate in the February 2006 municipal elections. This was stated in the global report of the State Department.[7] The US has also discontinued lethal arms aid to RNA since the royal takeover. According to the Foreign Operations Appropriations Act, 'foreign military financing will only be made available to Nepal if the secretary of state certifies that the government of Nepal has restored civil liberties, is protecting human rights and has demonstrated, through dialogue with Nepal's political parties, a commitment to a clear timetable to restore multi-party democratic government consistent with the 1990 Nepalese constitution.'[8] After a series of violent anti-King protests on the streets of Kathmandu, the United States asked the King on 11 April to start a dialogue with political parties and branded his takeover on 1 February 2005 as 'having failed in every regard'.[9] The visit of a delegation of American congressmen led by Dennis Hastert, speaker of the House of Representatives was cancelled.[10] The American Embassy closed its consular section and library and evacuation of non-

---

7. *The Himalayan,* 7 April '06.
8. Letter by Robert L. Hugins, public affairs officer, US Embassy, *The Kathmandu Post,* 5 April '06.
9. *The New York Times,* 12 April '06.
10. *The Kathmandu Post,* 13 April '06.

essential staff in mid April 2006. This was presumably done in view of the worsening security situation in Kathmandu after indefinite strikes and curfews. The proposed visit of former President Carter in early May was also cancelled because of the deteriorating situation in Kathmandu. It was expected that he would play a mediating role during his trip to Nepal.

11

A Failed State in the Making?

*The 1 February step in Nepal was necessitated by ground realities,
mainly the failure of successive governments to contain ever-
emboldening terrorists and maintain law and order. It has not come
at the cost of democracy, as some tend to project it. We remind the
international community of the pre-1 February situation in Nepal.
Our friends and well-wishers were warning us of the danger of
Nepal turning into a failed state.*
King Gyanendra, addressing the SAARC conference
in Dhaka, (12 November 2005)

*If armed Maoists and unarmed parties successfully implement
Prachanda's and Baburam Bhattarai's vision of a violent revolution
the Maoists will ultimately seize power and Nepal will suffer a
disaster that will make its current problems pale in comparison.*
James F. Moriarty, American ambassador to Nepal,
(*The Kathmandu Post*, 16 February 2006)

Profound change is now inevitable in Nepal. Nepal in 2006 is a country in crisis. There has never been such a crisis in its history ever since it was unified. Nobody knows what form it will take and in what direction it is headed. All three major actors, the monarch, political parties and the Maoists are responsible for this state of affairs. What started as an insignificant communist movement in the backward mid-western hills of Nepal in 1996, has now become a threat to the 237-year monarchy and has adversely affected parliamentary democracy by making holding of elections almost an impossible task in view of the armed insurgency. It could have been avoided had all three actors behaved responsibly.

Nepal is one of the least developed among the developing countries designated by the United Nations. The concern that Nepal might be heading towards being labelled a failed state was expressed at an international meeting on Nepal organised in London in June 2002. Nepal still had a functioning multi-party parliamentary democracy at that time and Prime Minister Deuba had just dissolved Parliament and called for elections to be held by November. Both of Nepal's neighbours, the USA, the UK, Russia, France, Germany, the World Bank and other multilateral agencies participated in the meeting. It was just a year after the royal massacre and British officials were worried that Nepal's fragile democracy might not be able to survive without some outside gestures of support.[1] The number of people killed had now reached the figure of 4,300.[2] Nepal had indicated in the

---

1. *The Kathmandu Post,* 21 June '02.
2. *The Kathmandu Post,* 20 May ''02.

conference that the tourism industry in the country was devastated and the country had suffered damages and revenue loss because of Maoist attack on civilian infrastructure. The meeting said that Nepal was facing 'an unprecedented crisis'. Things have worsened since then, as the number of people killed in early 2006 was 13,000.

American Deputy Assistant Secretary of State for South Asian Affairs Donald Camp has written how a Maoist victory in Nepal would be hostile to the US. According to him, it would destabilise the whole region and Nepal could easily turn into a failed state and become a potential haven for terrorists as in Afghanistan.[3] Kul C. Gautam, a Nepali national working as Undersecretary General for UNICEF in New York gave a presentation in Nepal in his personal capacity about the insurgency. He cautioned that Nepal should learn from the experience of other failed states who are reluctant to take external support.[4]

The Asian Centre for Human Rights (ACHR) said in a report that Nepal was facing the gravest humanitarian and human rights crisis in South Asia as 400,000 Nepalese were displaced from their villages.[5] The United Nations appealed for sixty-five million dollars in humanitarian aid by the end of 2005 that could put the country in the same boat as Chechnya, Palestine and twelve African nations. All of these are receiving assistance under Consolidated Appeals Process

---

3. Remarks to the Heritage Foundation, 3 March '03.
4. Gautam, Kul C., 'Possible Role of the UN in Peace Process in Nepal', *Annual Journal of Nepal Council of World Affairs, 2004-05*.
5. *DPA*, 14 March '05.

(CAP) in 2005. It said it could label the country as a 'failed state'.[6]

Tourism is one of the main foreign exchange earners in Nepal. There were several travel advisories from tourist generating countries due to the insurgency in the country. The number of tourists in the major trekking areas such as Everest Base Camp and the Annapurna area declined due to concerns about security and imposition of 'tax' by the Maoists. Many businesses dependent upon tourism suffered losses and many hotel rooms remained unoccupied. Several hotels in Kathmandu, such as Blue Star and Narayani, were converted into department stores. Hotels in Pokhara suffered greatly due to a decline in the number of tourists. Many entrepreneurs had invested in the hospitality industry by taking bank loans. A few in Pokhara and also along the major trekking trails had difficulty paying back interest on the loans. As the tourism industry was adversely affected, it created a multiplier effect in the whole economy. Many tourist entrepreneurs and even some tourists visiting Nepal joined in the protest to bring democracy in April 2006 in the touristy Thamel area of Kathmandu.

Islamic militants executed twelve Nepalese working in Iraq in September 2004. There were retaliatory attacks against mosques in Nepal, the first time such incidents had taken place. Offices of manpower agencies responsible for sending Nepalis to work in the Gulf countries were attacked. Nepal earns more than one billion dollars as remittance of Nepalese working overseas, mainly in the Gulf. If the Gulf countries

---

6. Logan, Marty, *Nepal: On the Road to Failed State*, *IPS*, 6 October '05.

had reacted by sending the Nepalese working there home, the economy would have been affected adversely. Fortunately, this did not happen. Nepalese from the hills had worked for more than a century either in the British or Indian Army as Gurkha soldiers and also as domestic aides or as guards in the cities of India. Their salary and pension helped the economy of the hills where there was little cultivable land. They are now working in the countries of the Gulf and Malaysia mainly as unskilled labour. Some have also migrated to the US as documented aliens or as students although there are a few who have legal residential permits.

Nepal is also facing a crisis in its economy. The central bank estimated that the annual rate of inflation in 2006 could be more than seven percent. As the price of fuel — diesel, petrol and kerosene — had risen in view of the increase in the prices in the international market, the rate of inflation could be in double digits. The Asian Development Bank has estimated that the growth rate in GDP will be about two percent in 2006. It will be third lowest among the Asian countries. If the population growth rate were taken into account it might even be close to zero or even negative. This is in contrast to its two neighbouring countries, India, which has a growth rate of 7.6 percent and China with 9.5 percent forecasted for 2006.[7] All of this could make the economic outlook very pessimistic. Government expenditure is also increasing without growth in revenue. A well-known economist, Raghav Dhoj Pant stated that Nepal could become bankrupt by mid 2006. He warned that the economy might collapse abruptly.

---

7. *The Kathmandu Post*, 7 April '06.

Nepal is also facing the problem of strikes called by agitating political parties and the Maoists that cause the economic activities to come to a standstill sometimes in the entire country or in certain parts depending upon where they are called. The government has also imposed curfew to maintain law and order not only in the capital city but also in many towns across the valley. Both curfews and strikes called by the government and the political parties caused considerable harm to the economy in the first and second week of April 2006. Actually, the SPA, which had called a four-day strike to agitate for democracy, announced it would call a strike indefinitely after the government-imposed curfew during daytime for a few days. The Maoists had also blockaded Kathmandu valley for several days in 2005 and 2006. There were times when vehicles had to be escorted to and from Kathmandu valley to ensure security from Maoist attacks. This has caused considerable loss to businesses and inconvenience to consumers because items such as vegetables and cooking gas being brought from the Terai were either not available in the market or were being sold at very high prices.

It is also possible that certain factors that helped make Nepal a terrorist hub in the 1990s also contributed in Nepal moving towards being a failed state. This was written as far back as 1994, two years before the start of insurgency: 'They have found a suitable environment in Nepal in view of long open border between Nepal and India, a weak government, widespread poverty and corruption in bureaucracy which has made smuggling of arms and gold relatively easy'.[8]

8. Raj, Prakash A., *Road to Kathmandu*, Nabeen Publications, Kathmandu, 1994.

In a nutshell, there were several factors that were contributing in making Nepal a failed state. Large parts of the country, especially rural areas under the control of the Maoists and the lack of a solution to the insurgency, was a political factor in causing the failed state syndrome. On the other hand, galloping inflation, shortfall in revenue collection, stopping of foreign aid, people being forced to pay taxes to the state as well as to the Maoists, were the economic factors contributing to making Nepal a failed state.

Maoist Supreme Leader Prachanda has suggested to the SPA to reinstate the Parliament dissolved in 2002 on the recommendation of Prime Minister Deuba. He had asked them to form a multi-party government to hold elections to the Constituent Assembly. According to him, the king would then be illegal. An interim government will be formed including the Maoists.[9] What Prachanda is suggesting is a parallel government in Nepal. Parallel governments are formed only in countries that become failed states due to civil war. The very fact that the Maoists and SPA, which held ninety percent of the seats in Parliament dissolved in 2002, have agreed to an accord and that one party proposing a parallel government, is indicative of Nepal already being a failed state. James F. Moriarty has commented on the proposal to form a parallel government with a parallel army as follows. 'A parallel government, with a parallel army? This is a recommendation that the political parties join the Maoists in the underground, violent struggle against the state — a formula to expand the bloodshed and misery in Nepal for the advantage of the Maoists, not to seek a peaceful, negotiated

9. *The Hindu*, 9 February '06.

settlement of the conflict'.[10] The Maoists have already established their own government in some rural areas imposing taxes and have a budget of their own. They also have a judicial system in the form of 'People's Court'. If they could convince the SPA to declare a parallel government in Kathmandu after restoring the dissolved Parliament, in which they will also participate, it could only be a matter of time before Nepal becomes engulfed in a full-scale civil war and is a 'failed state'.

10. Speech made by Ambassador Moriarty at a programme jointly organised by Ganesh Man Singh Academy and the American Center in Kathmandu on 15 February '06, reproduced in *The Telegraph Weekly*, 22 February '06.

12

The Indian Mess-up

Multi-party democracy was restored in Nepal after the success of the People's Movement in April 1990. Nepal had experimented with multi-party democracy for eighteen months when Prime Minister B.P. Koirala was elected after general elections in 1958 resulted in a two-thirds majority for Nepali Congress in Parliament. However, he was dismissed by King Mahendra in December 1960. King Mahendra began the party-less Panchayat system, which continued after his death in 1972 when his eldest son Birendra succeeded him. The period of 1988-89 was one of great economic problems for Nepal because of the blockade imposed by India as the existing Trade and Transit Treaty had expired.

The People's Movement dismantled the Panchayat system and sovereignty was transferred to the people. Krishna Prasad

Bhattarai was appointed prime minister during the interim period when the new 1990 Constitution was drafted, envisaging a parliamentary system of government for Nepal. There were three general elections in Nepal between 1991 and 1999; the Nepali Congress won a majority in the first and the third elections. There were three prime ministers from the Nepali Congress during this period: Girija Prasad Koirala, Krishna Prasad Bhattarai and Sher Bahadur Deuba. However, CPN (UML) emerged as the largest party in Parliament and Manmohan Adhikari was appointed prime minister. His tenure was to last for nine months.

Post the new Constitution in 1990, up to the removal of Deuba as prime minister in 2001, Indo-Nepal relations remained cordial. India and Nepal signed a trade treaty in 1996, when I.K. Gujral was prime minister, granting duty-free access for all Nepali goods into the Indian market. India also agreed to provide an alternative transit route from Nepal to Bangladesh in 1997. Prime Minister A.B. Vajpayee made the Indo-Nepal transit treaty renewable automatically every seven years, guaranteeing Nepal's access to sea in perpetuity.[1]

India had security concerns, however, owing to the prevailing lack of good governance, politicisation of bureaucracy and intelligence, and corruption in Nepal during this period. Contrary to Prof. S.D. Muni's statement that monarchy as an institution had done precious little in accommodating legitimate security and economic interests and concerns in Nepal[2], it was post 1990 that such activities

---

1. Rajan, K.V., 'Nepal', in *External Affairs: Cross-Border Relations*, ed. by J.N. Dixit.
2. Muni, S.D., *Maoist Insurgency in Nepal*, Rupa & Co., New Delhi, 2003.

became more common as compared to the Panchayat period when the monarch was all-powerful.

India's concerns were clearly not unfounded. Funds and logistic support behind the blasts that shook Mumbai in early 1993, months after the Babri Masjid in Ayodhya was demolished by Hindu militants, were possibly channelled via Nepal. An armed Indian police group raided a house in Baneshwar area, in the heart of Kathmandu, in March 1994 to arrest an Indian terrorist. In August 1994, Mr Chavan, the Home minister of India, announced the arrest of Yakub Memon, one of the main suspects in the Mumbai blasts. The accused claimed that he had been arrested in Nepal and handed over to the Indians.[3] An Indian weekly gave details of Memon's arrest in Kathmandu, saying, 'The principal staging point for terrorist attacks on India by Pakistan's Inter Services Intelligence is now Kathmandu.'[4] One Nepali weekly quoting the Central Bureau of Investigation wrote that a member of the Nepali Parliament was involved in the Mumbai blasts.[5] M.D. Nalapat of *The Times of India* wrote that a powerful lobby within the Nepali Congress was being cultivated by the Pakistan Embassy in Kathmandu, with the aim of trying to unseat Girija Koirala.[6] He also wrote that Pakistan was rapidly gaining adherents among Bangladeshi infiltrators and that madrasas were mushrooming along the border. The then Indian ambassador to Nepal, he said, was

---

3. Raj, Prakash A., *Road to Kathmandu*, Nabeen, Kathmandu, 1994.
4. Gupta, *Sunday*, 14 August 1994.
5. *Deshantar*, 8 November 1995.
6. Nalapat, M.D., 'Not Much Ado about Kathmandu', *The Times of India*, 28 August 1994.

adopting a very low profile which was not being received well by some officials in the embassy.

When Manmohan Adhikari visited India in 1995, he said he supported India's security concerns completely but he was not in favour of a 'security umbrella'.[7] He proposed that some kind of 'record keeping' be set up at the Indo-Nepal border, so the movement of people could be monitored.[8]

Another instance of a major security lapse was the December 1999 hijacking of an Indian Airlines aircraft flying to New Delhi from Kathmandu. The Islamic militants who had taken over the plane flew to Kandahar in Taliban-ruled Afghanistan. The Indian foreign minister Jaswant Singh flew to Kandahar and after negotiations, gave up three militants jailed in India in exchange for the passengers.

The hijacking episode demonstrated how Nepalese territory was being used to conduct terrorist acts against a friendly neighbour — India. In view of terrorist attacks in the Indian Parliament and temples, there seem to be organisations and countries that are inimical to the existence of India and the open border existing between Nepal and India. That one can travel without passport, visa or identity card between the two countries seems to facilitate these problems.[9] Two Pakistan embassy officials were arrested in Nepal under charges of being in possession of RDX explosives and fake Indian currency, but were released as they claimed diplomatic immunity.[10]

---

7. *The Times of India*, 10 April 1995.
8. *The Times of India*, 12 April 1995.
9. Raj, Prakash A., 'Monitoring the Indo-Nepal Border', *The People's Review*, 13 March '03.
10. Raj, Prakash A., 'Playing Cat and Mouse in Kathmandu', *Nepali Times*, 20 April '01.

It is important to remember, in this context, the US State Department report on terrorism which states: 'Limited government finances, weak border controls and poor security infrastructure have made Nepal a convenient logistic and transit point for some outside militants and international terrorists. The country also possesses a number of relatively soft targets that make it a potentially attractive site for terrorist operation'.[11]

Employment in the Gulf region and Malaysia now constitute one of the major sources of foreign exchange earnings for Nepal. This is in contrast to the situation in the 1970s and 1980s, when a large number of Nepalese were employed either in the Indian Gurkha army or as domestic help in India. The number of Nepalese students studying in India has also declined in recent years.

India and the Royal Massacre

Although an investigation commission set up by King Gyanendra points to Crown Prince Dipendra as the assassin in the Royal massacre of 2001, there are still many who doubt the authenticity of the report. The Maoist leader, Baburam Bhattarai, blames Indian and American intelligence networks, RAW and CIA, for the killings; his only crime, he says, are his liberal views.[12] It is interesting to note that Nepal was a constitutional monarchy at the time, and had a functioning

---

11. US Department of State, Annual Report on Patterns of Global Terrorism, 2003.
12. Raj, Prakash A., *Kay Gardeko: The Royal Massacre in Nepal*, Rupa & Co. New Delhi, 2001.

multi-party democratic system. However, Girija Prasad Koirala, the then prime minister, had a minimal role to play in appointing the investigation commission. In fact, he was informed of the massacre hours after it had happened.

Immediately after the massacre, India's Cabinet Committee on Security met. The Indian government decided to support King Gyanendra as he had the support of the army, and the ruling Koirala government.[13] At a briefing organised by the Ministry of External Affairs a few days after the Royal massacre, the Indian government was reported to have stated that it was against playing a pro-active role. A former Indian ambassador to Nepal, A.R. Deo, is reported to have said that the major concern would be how India's security would be affected after the incident. As the Pakistani envoy in Nepal had reportedly called Islamabad to give them the news that the perpetrator of the massacre was none other than Dipendra, twelve hours before the official announcement, the Indian government was made aware of the 'level of Islamabad's penetration into the palace'.[14]

13. Gupta, Shishir, 'India's Response, Walking the Tightrope', *India Today*, 18 June '01.
14. Sudarshan, V., 'Till Kingdom Come', *Outlook*, 18 June '01.

13

The King Succumbs to Pressure

When King Gyanendra dismissed Sher Bahadur Deuba on 1 February 2005, there were different kinds of reactions from the international community. The king had, however, for all practical purposes taken over the government three years back, in October 2002, when he had dismissed Sher Bahadur Deuba for the first time after the latter's failure to conduct elections for Parliament within six months of its dissolution. There was not much adverse reaction internationally in 2002, however, as the king had quickly appointed two former prime ministers, Surya Bahadur Thapa and Lokendra Bahadur Chand, who had nominated several people with a background in politics.

Deuba's second dismissal, however, drew strong reactions internationally. The king's reason for dismissing Deuba this time, was corruption. The former prime minister was even imprisoned by the newly-formed Royal Corruption Control. The king then went on to form a ministry under his own chairmanship on 1 February 2005, which included two vice-chairmen, Tulsi Giri and Kirti Nidhi Bista, both in their late seventies, who had both been prime ministers some thirty years earlier under the Panchayat system. Emergency was then imposed on the country. Prime Minister Manmohan Singh of India reacted to this saying the step represented 'a setback to democracy'. India was worried the Maoists would gain from the chaos that was sure to ensue.[1]

According to *The Indian Express*, the king was well aware of what India's reaction would be to his forming a ministry under his own chairmanship, and by taking the step anyway, he was sending out a message. He is also reported to have ignored India's advice that the king and political leaders try and work out a compromise.[2] However, India's Defence Minister Pranab Mukherjee said India would continue to have longstanding ties with the Royal Nepal Army.[3]

The Government of India decided to stop their supply of arms to Nepal. The Nepalese Foreign Minister Ramesh Nath Pandey, while visiting Delhi a month after the coup, was told that Delhi stopped military supplies 'because it was wary of such equipment going to the wrong hands'. MEA's spokes-person said, 'We are not sure whether it is going to strengthen security forces in Nepal or the Maoists. That's why we stopped military supplies.'[4] A columnist in an Indian newspaper wrote

1. *The Asian Age*, 2 February '05.
2. *The Indian Express*, 6 February '06.
3. *The Indian Express*, 10 February '06.
4. *The Kathmandu Post*, 8 March '05.

that such arguments as Maoists in Nepal are more of a threat to India than the king, are without foundation, and the king's disposition towards India is suspect.[5] He wrote that India had huge stakes in the stability and security of Nepal, and that India's national security objectives also included state failure and the emergence of an extremist government in Kathmandu.[6]

The United States, too, reacted sharply to the king's move. Spokesman of the State Department, Richard Boucher, said a declaration of a state of emergency and suspension of fundamental constitutional rights and dismissal of a multi-party government was a step back from democracy.[7] James F. Moriarty, said there was pressure from the US Congress and the American public on the king to try and reach out to the political parties. He said the king had given a time frame of three months to 'straighten the stuff out'.[8] The United States pulled out all non-essential staff from Nepal and closed the consular section at Kathmandu a week after the start of the SPA-sponsored strike.[9]

The United Kingdom too joined in the voices against this setback to democracy, threatening to withdraw economic assistance to Nepal. They did in fact suspend military assistance to Nepal. Pakistan, on the other hand offered to supply arms to Nepal.[10]

5. Sahay, Anand K., 'Kings and Commies', *The Times of India,* 16 February '05.
6. Raja Mohan, C., 'With Neighbours like These, *The Indian Express,* 8 February '05.
7. News Release, American Center, US Embassy, 2 February '05.
8. *The Kathmandu Post,* 12 February '05.
9. *The Himalayan Times,* 14 April '06.
10. *The Times of India,* 15 March '05.

The European Union said it was in favour of a broad-based government.

China, however, remained diplomatic, stating that a Royal coup was an internal matter for Nepal.

Nepalese Finance Minister Madhukar Rana said that countries were setting such conditions as withdrawal of the state of emergency, restoration of freedom of expression and release of detained political activists to resume aid.[11]

Despite all this reaction from the international community, it was felt that perhaps India was not doing enough. India's National Security Advisor M.K. Narayanan said India's Nepal policy had not been very successful and it was not 'putting as much pressure' on the king 'as possible'.[12]

King Gyanendra's first royal proclamation after the SPA strike on 20 April was after his meeting with Dr. Karan Singh, special envoy of the Indian prime minister, Dr.Manmohan Singh. As Karan Singh is the son of Maharaja Hari Singh, the last ruler of Kashmir, his choice as an envoy at a crucial time in Nepal's history might have played a role in persuading the king to hand over executive power. James F. Moriarty had warned on the day of the first Royal Proclamation that King Gyanendra 'will lose his kingdom' if didn't act quickly to end the crisis. He had also said earlier in an interview to CNN that the king might have to flee the country clinging to the undercarriage of a helicopter if he didn't back down. The ambassador was later called to the Nepalese Foreign Ministry to explain himself.

---

11. *The Kathmandu Post*, 10 March '05.
12. *The Kathmandu Post*, 21 March '05.

The king said in his proclamation that he was returning executive power which he had taken on 1 February 2005 to the people and invited the SPA to recommend the name of a prime minister. India, the US and the countries of the EU and the UK welcomed the step. However, Indian Foreign Secretary Shyam Sharan later said that the proclamation was not enough.

The Indian ambassador to Nepal was reported to have met the king on the day of the second royal proclamation in which he agreed to reinstate the dissolved House of Representatives. Not only did he reinstate the dissolved House but he also accepted the road map of the Twelve-Point Accord that had been signed between the SPA and the Maoists. It appears that persuasion by the Indian Foreign secretary and former ambassador to Nepal played a role in this. The unusual delay in responding to the crisis in Nepal could have been contributory factors in foreign 'pressure' on him. When more than half a million demonstrators had come out on the Ring Road — in defiance of a curfew — many foreign countries might have concluded that either the king had to hand over power to the SPA or lose his kingdom. If, after 1 February 2005, the royal government had been able to show that some progress was being made in resolving the Maoist issue, it is possible that foreign countries such as the US would have supported the king.

In addition to the large number of protesters in the streets, such factors as defiance of curfew, joining of anti-government protests by civil servants from such sensitive ministries as the Cabinet Secretariat and Home Ministry might also have tilted the balance against the king in the eyes of the foreign envoys.

Meeting of the Restored Parliament

The demand for restoration of Parliament elected under the 1990 Constitution in 1999 and dissolved three years later in May 2002, was on the agenda of the SPA. It was included in the Twelve-Point Agreement between SPA and CPN (Maoist). King Gyanendra had to accede to this demand in the Royal Proclamation given on 24 April 2006 as the Jana Andolan or People's Movement had gathered momentum and a gathering of two million people was planned in Kathmandu the next day, which could have marched to the Narayanhiti Royal Palace.

The decision to restore Parliament was a political one and had no legal basis as the tenure of Parliament elected in 1999 would have expired in 2004 had it not been dissolved legally. The Supreme Court had approved the dissolution as being legal and in accordance to the Constitution. The restoration owed its existence solely due to the *widespread support for,* and *success of,* the Jana Andolan. It owed its success also to the participation of a large number of Maoists in the rallies in the capital city. Girija Prasad Koirala's name was recommended by the SPA for prime minister. The eighty-four-year-old Nepali Congres leader was too sick either to take oath of his office or attend the first meeting of restored Parliament on 28 April 2006. It's a mystery why the SPA recommended his name and not that of any younger leader for such a post at such a crucial moment in the country's history. The Maoist supreme leader Prachanda issued a statement and declared a unilateral ceasefire from 26 April. He also called off economic blockade of district headquarters throughout the country. He gave a two-day deadline to begin the process of re-writing the Constitution.[1]

On 30 April 2006, G.P. Koirala was finally sworn in as prime minister of Nepal by King Gyanendra at the Royal Palace. The swearing-in had been postponed earlier due to Koirala's ill health. Some said he was suffering from bronchitis. Others suspected it was something more serious. One physician accompanied him on his trip to the palace. Koirala didn't take oath as a member of Raj Sabha, a kind of royal privy council as he had done four times earlier. He formed his Cabinet two days later and appointed K.P. Sharma Oli from CPN (UML) as deputy prime minister and minister of Foreign Affairs. Other ministers included Krishna Sitaula from Nepali Congress as Home minister and Ram Sharan Mahat from Nepali Congress as Finance minister. There was reported to be considerable discussions before the names of Cabinet ministers was finalised. Two constituent parties of SPA declined to nominate a member in the Cabinet. It was reported that CPN (UML) wanted the Home portfolio and it was not agreeable to Nepali Congress because of its sensitive nature as the police would have been under it. The restored House of Representatives passed a resolution unanimously on 30 April, the proposal for elections for a Constituent Assembly.

Tara Nath Rana Bhat, the speaker of Parliament in 1999 had continued to hold his post even after its dissolution in May 2002. However, he had not joined the movement of the SPA against autocratic monarchy. There were demands in the party that he should resign from his post and he did so just before the convening of Parliament. He had held the post

1. *The Himalayan Times*, 29/4/06.

for six years including almost four years when the Parliament was non-existent. Chitra Lekha Yadav, a Madheshi woman from eastern Terai whose first language was Maithili, chaired the first meeting of the restored House. Although it was not planned that way and was a coincidence, the person chairing the meeting was from a community and gender that had not been part of the mainstream in more than two centuries of post unification Nepal. It was perhaps, symbolic of the advent of a new era of inclusive democracy. It was customary to place a royal scepter in the House at an appointed place behind the speaker before the beginning of the session. This was not done this time.

Girija Koirala, the newly appointed prime minister sent a motion calling for elections to the Constituent Assembly, declare a cease-fire with the Maoists and hold talks with them. He was too sick to attend the session himself. Members of civil society, youth and human rights activists encircled the Secretariat complex in Singha Durbar, formerly the palace of Ranas that was converted into the Secretariat of the government where the Parliament building is also situated. They were asking for "unconditional constitutional assembly".[2] Sitaram Yechuri, leader of CPM in India also attended the meeting of Parliament as a guest.

The Maoists held an open meeting at the open-air theater in the heart of Kathmandu. Lekh Nath Nuepane, president of the Maoist student wing of All Nepal National Independent Student's Union accused the SPA of having committed a "historic blunder" in concluding mass movement with an agreement with the royal palace under the influence of

2. *The Kathmandu Post*, 29/4/06.

"imperialists and expansionists". Another leader called the restoration of Parliament as an act of the deception.

A meeting of SPA including Nepali Congress, CPN-UML has proposed replacing "His Majesty's Government" with "Nepal Government", making the prime minister instead of the king as the supreme commander-in-chief and to replace the current national anthem that glorifies the king. Above all, it was proposed to keep the army under Parliament instead of the king.[3] It seems probable that Nepal would become a "secular" state instead of a "Hindu" state after elections to a Constituent Assembly.

Nepal is thus at the threshold of an epoch-making change. However, some questions remain unanswered as to whether the Maoists will disarm before holding elections for constituent assembly and respect its verdict. Would peace finally return to Nepal?

One of the first decisions of newly formed Cabinet was to declare ceasefire by the government for indefinite period of time. The Maoists had declared a three-month ceasefire few days earlier. The government also removed Interpol Red Corner notice on insurgent leaders. The results of municipal elections held in February by the Royal government were also declared null and void. American Assistant Secretary of State for South Asian and Central Asian Affairs Richard Boucher visited Kathmandu for two days and met Prime Minister Koirala and COAS Thapa and leaders of political parties but didn't meet the king. He said the US would support the economic and security needs.

---

3. *Kantipur*, 27/4/06.

Appendix 1

People Who Matter in Nepal Now

Acharya, Narahari

Narahari Acharya was a teacher of Nepali at the university before joining politics as a member of the Nepali Congress. He has been quite vocal against absolute monarchy and was one of the first NC leaders to advocate a new Constitution to be made by a Constituent Assembly. He also contested for the post of president of the party against Girija Koirala and was defeated. He was imprisoned for several months by the government after the Royal takeover.

Acharya, Shailaja

She is the niece of B.P. Koirala and Girija Koirala and is a second-generation leader of the Nepali Congress and the Koirala family. She served briefly as minister of agriculture in the first Nepali Congress Government in 1991 and was appointed deputy prime minister in 1998 when her uncle became prime minister for the second time. She has a 'clean' image unlike some other leaders of the Nepali Congress.

Adhikari, Bharat Mohan

He is a younger brother of late Man Mohan Adhikari, the first Communist prime minister of Nepal. He belongs to CPN (UML) and was appointed deputy prime minister in 2004 when Sher Bahadur Deuba was appointed prime minister again after his dismissal in October 2002. He had also served as minister of Finance in 1994-95 when his brother was prime minister.

Adhikari, Dhrub

He is a well-known journalist of Nepal and has been BBC's Nepal correspondent for some time.

Badal, Ram Bahadur Thapa

Badal is the *nom de plume* of Ram Bahadur Thapa who belongs to the Magar ethnic group from Gulmi district in the western hills of Nepal. His parents were serving in the Indian Army. He also studied in the Soviet Union in late 1970s. He is the main military strategist of the Maoists.

Banstola, Chakra

He comes from an affluent family in Ilam in the eastern hills and represented Jhapa in the parliamentary elections held in 1999. He served as minister of Tourism and Foreign Affairs in the Nepali Congress government.

Baral, Lok Raj

Baral was professor of political science at Tribhuwan University and was appointed Nepalese ambassador to India. He is apparently close to the Nepali Congress Party. He has also written some books on governance.

Bhattarai, Baburam

Bhattarai is one of two most important Maoist leaders. He is the foremost intellectual in the Maoist movement. He was born in a middle class Brahmin family in the village of Khoplang in Gorkha district and was educated in a missionary school in Nepal and at Jawaharlal Nehru University in India.

Bhattarai, Krishna Prasad

Bhattarai is one of the founding members of the Nepali Congress and was also a member of the troika consisting of Ganesh Man Singh and Girija Prasad Koirala that succeeded B.P. Koirala in leadership. He was appointed prime minister in the Interim Government in April 1990 after the restoration of multi-party democracy. He could not continue in the post as he lost the 1991 elections. However, he became prime minister one more time. Although in his eighties, he still has influence among party members.

Bhattarai, Rajan

Rajan Bhattarai is one of young emerging leaders of CPN (UML). He was for some time with the Foreign Policy cell of UML. He was reportedly sent abroad to lobby for the party after the Royal takeover in 2005.

Bista, Kirti Nidhi

Kirti Nidhi Bista was prime minister of Nepal three times during the Panchayat era under the kingship of both King Mahendra and King Birendra. He was appointed vice chairman of the Council of Ministers in 2005 after the Royal takeover by King Gyanendra. A staunch loyalist, he is also well known for his integrity.

Budhamagar, Santosh

He is the chief of 'Magarat Autonomous Region' created by the Maoists in western hills. He is a member of the Maoist Politbureau.

Bogati, Post Bahadur, 'Diwakar'

He is a Maoist leader from Nuwakot. His son was killed during army operations. He is a member of the Politbureau and Standing Committee.

Chand, Lokendra Bahadur

Lokendra Bahadur Chand has the distinction of becoming prime minister during the Panchayat era, during the multi-party system and again after the Royal takeover. He comes from the remote hilly district of Baitadi in the far west of Nepal.

Chaudhary, Parashu Narayan

He belongs to the backward Tharu ethnic group and comes from Dang. He was originally a member of Nepali Congress and was included in B.P. Koirala's Cabinet formed in 1959. He later joined Panchayat after the royal coup in 1960. He was appointed as chairman of the Standing Committee of Rajya Sabha by King Gyanendra.

Deuba, Arzoo

Arzoo Deuba married Sher Bahadur Deuba when he was already prime minister of Nepal. She is the great granddaughter of Rana Prime Minister Juddha Shamsher. She was working in INGOS prior to her marriage.

Deuba, Sher Bahadur

Sher Bahadur Deuba has enjoyed several distinctions in Nepali politics since 1996. He was appointed prime minister three times, including twice during the multi-party system. He was not very well known till 1991 when he was appointed Home minister in the Ministry headed by Girija Prasad Koirala. He was later appointed prime minister. It was during his tenure that the Maoist Insurgency started and it was to him that they presented their forty-point demands. He was re-appointed prime minister and it was he who recommended the dissolution of House of Representatives in May 2002 although the tenure of Parliament elected in 1999 was not completed. As it was not possible to hold polls within six months, King Gyanendra dismissed him and called him 'incompetent'. He was called again and appointed prime minister in 2004 and dismissed again by the king before he took over on 1 February 2005. He was imprisoned for about a year on charges of corruption by the Royal Commission. The Commission was later declared unconstitutional by the Supreme Court and Deuba was released. He is the chairman of Nepali Congress (Democratic), a break-away group from Nepali Congress.

Dhungana, Daman
Daman Dhungana was the Speaker of first House of Representatives elected in 1990 from Nepali Congress. He was defeated from his constituency in Kathmandu in the 1994 elections. He was appointed as a 'facilitator' during Government-Maoist talks in 2003.

Gautam, Bamdev
Gautam was deputy prime minister and Home minister in an UML-RPP coalition government. He later joined a break-away group CPN (ML). He is a Brahmin from the mid-western hill district of Piuthan.

Giri, Pradip
He is an intellectual in Nepali Congress (now with Nepali Congress Democratic). He represented a constituency in eastern Terai although he is originally from the hills. He was closely associated with B.P. Koirala during his exile in Banaras in the 1970s.

Giri, Tulsi
Giri was a close associate of Prime Minister B.P. Koirala when the latter was dismissed by King Mahendra in 1960. He collaborated with the king and joined his Cabinet in 1961 as vice chairman. After a few years he was dropped. He was appointed prime minister by King Birendra during Panchayat years. Giri was a member of the Hindu organisation Rashtriya Swayamsevak Sangh (RSS) during his student days in India. He later converted to Christianity (Jehova's Witness) and went to live in Sri Lanka. However, King Gyanendra called him back after he took over on 1 February 2005 and appointed him deputy chairman in his Council of Ministers.

Gurung, Dev

He is a member of the Maoist Politbureau and chief of Tamuwan Autonomous Region. He is from the Manang district in the north, which is unaffected by the insurgency. He was a member of the Maoist negotiating team that came to Kathmandu in 2003. He is married to Yashoda Subedi, a Maoist leader.

Gurung, Harka

Dr Harka Gurung is a geographer of international repute in Nepal. He has served as vice chairman of the Planning Commission and minister during Panchayat years. He has also worked for the United Nations. He has been leading a movement in recent years to declare Nepal as a secular state and for drafting a new Constitution by a Constitutional Assembly in which the rights of Janjatis will be assured. Many Janjatis in Nepal now follow Hinduism and speak Nepali as their first language. Gurung tried to persuade the Janjatis to declare Buddhism as their religion and a language other than Nepali as their first language during the 2001 Census.

Gurung, Om

Om Gurung is a professor at Tribhuwan University. He is also chairman of Federation of Nationalities (*Janajati Mahasangha*).

Gyawali, Chandra Kant

He is a bright young lawyer who has filed many public interest litigations at the Supreme Court that have resulted in several decisions affecting polygamy, citizenship, prison reforms, etc.

Gyawali, Hem Raj

He is chairman of Kantipur Group of Publications publishing such newspapers as *Kantipur* (the largest circulated daily in Nepali) and *The Kathmandu Post*. He also owns Kantipur Television. He comes from Gulmi in western hills.

Josse, Mana Ranjan
Josse is one of best- known journalists in Nepal and served as editor of *The Rising Nepal* during Panchayat days. He was later made deputy permanent representative of Nepal to the United Nations. Now he writes for *The People's Review*.

Katuwal, Rukmangad
Major General Katuwal is next in line to succeed Commander-in-Chief Pyar Jung Thapa sometime in 2006. He was in the National Security Council and was promoted to chief of General Staff in 2005.

Khanal, Jhala Nath
He is one of the senior leaders of CPN (UML) who was minister in the interim government formed in 1990. He is a Bahun and comes from Ilam in the eastern hills.

Koirala, Girija Prasad
Girija Prasad Koirala is the youngest brother of B.P. Koirala who was the first elected prime minister of Nepal. He also became the first prime minister to be elected after the restoration of multi-party democracy in 1991. He was appointed prime minister again in April 2006 after Jana Andolan as a nominee of SPA.

Koirala, Sujata
Sujata is the daughter of Girija Prasad Koirala. She is married to a German national named Jost. She has a keen interest in politics and is regarded as one of the contenders to take over leadership of the party.

Lal, C.K
Lal is an engineer from eastern Terai who writes on contemporary issues in *Nepali Times*.

Limbu, Gajendra Bahadur
He worked as principal military secretary to King Gyanendra from 2003-05.

Lohani, Prakash Chandra

He was minister both during the Panchayat days and also in the Nepali Congress-RPP coalition during multi-party democracy. He has a doctorate in economics from an American university, and was minister for Foreign Affairs and Finance at separate times. He is now in the Janashakti Party, a breakaway group of RPP.

Mahara, Krishna Bahadur

Mahara is a well-known Maoist leader who has participated in Government-Maoist peace talks held in Kathmandu. He was active in politics during his student days in P.N. College in Pokhara and also worked as a schoolteacher. His nom de plume is 'Amarsingh'. He is a Chhetri.

Maharjan, Pashupati

Pashupati Maharjan, a Newar from Kathmandu, is the principal secretary of King Gyanendra.

Mahat, Ram Sharan

A member of Nepali Congress, Mahat was elected to Parliament from Nuwakot district adjoining Kathmandu valley. He was twice appointed as minister of Finance. He has served for several years at UNDP offices in Kathmandu and also in Pakistan.

Mohsin, Mohammad

Mohsin is a bureaucrat turned politician and was associated with RPP. He was once minister of Tourism and comes from a Kashmiri Muslim family resident in Kathmandu for several centuries. He was appointed as minister again after October 2002 and was spokesperson of the government.

Nepal, Madhav Kumar

Nepal is a hill Brahmin resident in the Terai district of Rautahat. He served as deputy prime minister and foreign minister during the UML government in 1994. He was imprisoned for several months after the Royal takeover in 2005.

Oli, K.P. Sharma
Oli is a Brahmin from eastern hills living in the Terai district of Jhapa. He was minister of Home Affairs in the UML government in 1994 and is said to represent a faction in UML that is opposed to Madhav Kumar Nepal.

Pahadi, Krishna
He is one of most vocal opponents of the royal government and was imprisoned for several months after the Royal takeover. He is a well-known human rights activist and has spoken against human rights violations by both the state and the insurgents. He has worked in several human rights organisations.

Pandey, Devendra Raj
Pandey is a bureaucrat turned politician. He holds a doctorate from the US. He was also secretary of Finance, but resigned from his post. He was appointed minister of Finance in the interim government formed in 1990. He is one of the main opponents of King Gyanendra's regime and was detained for several months after the Royal takeover in 2005.

Pandey, Ramesh Nath
Pandey is a journalist turned politician. He has served as minister during the Panchayat days and after October 2002. His most recent assignment is minister for Foreign Affairs.

'Pasang' Nanda Kishor Pun
He is a well-known Maoist commander and is a member of the Politbureau. He was the Maoist commander during the attack on Beni in western hills resulting in the death of fourteen RNA soldiers and seventeen policemen. He is from Rolpa and was a teacher at one time.

Pokharel, Durga

Durga Pokhrel has been active in politics since her student days. She was a member of Nepali Congress Party. After getting her doctorate from Harvard, she lived in the US for more than a decade. After returning to Nepal she was appointed chairperson of the National Women's Commission. She was later appointed minister of state after the Royal takeover in 2005.

Pokhrel, Shankar

Pokhrel is one of the leaders of UML belonging to the new generation.

Pradhan, Sahana

Sahana Pradhan is the wife of late Pushpa Lal Shrestha, the founder of the Communist movement in Nepal. She served in the interim government formed after restoration of democracy in 1990. After the split in CPN (UML), she was elected chairperson of CPN (ML).

Pushpa Kamal Dahal 'Prachanda'

Prachanda or the 'feared one' is the *nom de plume* of the most important Maoist leader in Nepal. His family is originally from Pokhara valley; they migrated to Chitwan in the inner Terai in the Sixties. He studied agriculture at Rampur in Chitwan. His brand of Maoism is known as *Prachanda Path*. He is well known for his organisational capabilities.

Prashrit, Modnath (1942-)

Prashrit, a member of UML, had studied Sanskrit before joining the party. He is a Brahmin from western hills. He served as minister of Education in UML government in 1994.

Pun, Barsaman, 'Ananta'

He is a member of the Maoist Politbureau and was commander of eastern region. He is allegedly an expert in military strategy.

Rana Bhat, Tara Nath

Rana Bhat is a Chhetri from Pokhara. He was elected as Speaker of

Parliament in 1999. He has remained so for more than seven years despite dissolution of Parliament. He was the one who presented the report of the commission investigating the Royal massacre in 2001 to the Press.

Rana, Himalaya Shamsher

He spent several years working in the Nepalese civil service, the United Nations and served as UNDP resident representative at Afghanistan, Pakistan and Myanmar. He is one of the founding members of the Himalayan Bank in Kathmandu. He has taken part in several seminars regarding the Maoist insurgency.

Pun, Narayan Singh

He was appointed minister twice after October 2002. He was a member of the government negotiating team during a dialogue with the Maoists in 2003. He belongs to the Samata Party. He is from Myagdi district in western hills and is reportedly related to the Maoist leader Badal by marriage.

Rana, Pashupati Shamsher

He was minister for several years during the Panchayat era and also in coalition ministries after 1990. He is the grandson of the last Rana prime minister of Nepal. He is married to the daughter of Vijaya Raje Scindia of Gwalior in India. He is the father of Devayani Rana whom Crown Prince Dipendra wanted to marry, which triggered the Royal massacre of 2001. He is the first cousin of Dr Karan Singh's wife, who was the Indian prime minister's special envoy in April 2006.

Rana, Shirish Shamsher

He has served in the English language press in Nepal as a journalist and also entered politics as a member of a small political party. He was appointed minister of State for Information and spokesperson of the government after the Royal takeover in 2005.

Rana, Sachit Shamsher
Rana is a retired commaner-in-chief of Nepal. He is a member of Raj Sabha and has been quite vocal in supporting King Gyanendra. He is supposed to be one of his main advisors.

Rayamajhhi, Keshar Jung
He is one of the oldest communist leaders in Nepal and belongs to Palpa in western hills. He has often been called a Royal Communist as he supported monarchy. He was appointed minister in the interim government in 1990 and served as chairman of Standing Committee of Raj Sabha.

Rawal, Bhim
Rawal is a young leader of UML from the far western hills. He was minister of Tourism in UML ministry in 1994.

Rohit, Narayan Man Bijukachhe
Rohit is a charismatic leader from Bhaktpur and represents a Communist party called Nepal Peasants and Workers Party.

Sangraula, Khagendra
Sangraula is a left leaning Brahmin writer in Nepali language. His commentaries on the political scene published in Nepali language Press became very popular.

Shah, Sharad Chandra
Sharad Chandra Shah was quite powerful during the last phase of Panchayat years. His house in Kathmandu was burned down by demonstrators in April 1990. He returned to Nepal after living many years in self-imposed exile in Singapore. He belongs to the family of Salyani Rajas. Salyan was one of the principalities in mid-western hills whose Rajas did not fight the Gurkha conquest but collaborated and were able to maintain their autonomous status. His maternal grandfather was Kaiser Shamsher Rana. He is reported to be one of the main advisors of King Gyanendra.

Armed police force fighting against the demonstrators at Kalanki, 8 April 2006.

IOM students burning effigies of the members of the Royal government, Maharajgunj, 8 April 2006.

Lighting fires on the road to create obstacles for the police during curfew, 8 April 2006.

Police trying to extinguish fires lit by activists, 12 April 2006.

Doctors of Bir hospital (Nepal's first hospital) participating in the people's revolution, 13 April 2006.

Doctors treating the wounded at Bir hospital, 23 April 2006.

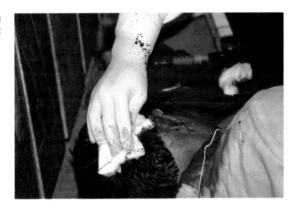

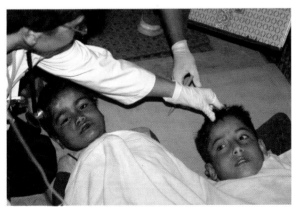

Dr Sarita Pandey (Model hospital) treating wounded children hurt at Tripureshwor, 23 April 2006.

Foreigners and human rights activists taking the wounded to Bir hospital, 23 April 2006.

Doctors in the Emergency department of the Teaching hospital treating those wounded while demonstrating against the curfew at Gogabu, 23 April 2006.

A man shot at Indra Chowk being taken to hospital by local activists.

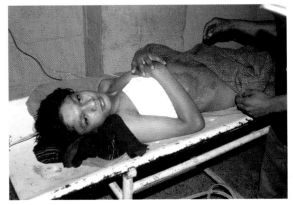

A fourteen-year-old boy being treated at Bir hospital, 23 April 2006.

Dr Sarita Pandey enquiring about the patient's condition, who was hit on the head by the police at Tripureshwar, 23 April 2006.

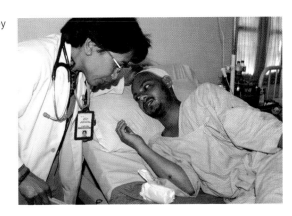

A youth scanning the list of injured, 25 April 2006.

Police clearing the area of demonstrators against the curfew that had been imposed, 10 April 2006.

Foreigners displaying placards and showing their solidarity to the people's movement, Thamel, 17 April 2006.

Dr Bryan treating the wounded policemen, 8 April 2006.

Foreigners supporting the people's movement at Jawakhel, Lalitpur, 12 April 2006.

At Gurukul, artists painting the signs of the victory of the people's movement, 25 April 2006.

Singers at the Gurukul singing the famous song (*gaun gaun bata utha...basti basti bata utha...*), from left Shyam Tamot, Ramesh Shrestha and Shyam Bhakta Shrestha, 25 April 2006.

Supreme Leader Ganesh Mansingh announcing the people's movement of 1990 at Chaksbari, National Conference, 18 February 1990.

Indian leader Chandrashekhar addressing the Nepali Congress meeting at Ganesh Mansingh Bhavan where the first day of the democracy movement was announced, 18 February 1990.

Shah, Gyanendra Bir Bikram

King Gyanendra has the distinction of being crowned twice in fifty years. He was crowned in 1950 when he was barely three years old when his grandfather King Tribhuwan had left Nepal for India, a step that led to the downfall of the Rana oligarchy. When King Tribhuwan returned to Nepal in February 1951, it marked the advent of democracy in Nepal. The second crowning of Gyanendra took place in June 2001, fifty years later, when his elder brother King Birendra and eight Royal relatives were massacred allegedly by Crown Prince Dipendra. Although in a coma, Dipendra was declared monarch, but he died three days later. Gyanendra was made regent and then crowned king. King Gyanendra was bound by the 1990 Constitution that gave nominal powers to the monarch. There was a functioning Parliament and Girija Prasad Koirala was the prime minister who enjoyed the confidence of Parliament. He was later succeeded by Sher Bahadur Deuba who asked for dissolution of Parliament in May 2002. When Deuba could not hold elections within six months of dissolution due to the Maoist insurgency, King Gyanendra dismissed him in October 2002. He appointed three prime ministers between October 2002 and January 2005 belonging to different political parties. However, he took over on 1 February 2005, appointing himself as chairman of Council of Ministers. He said he would hold elections within three years (i.e. before 2008) and hand back power to the elected representatives of the people. He imposed a state of emergency that was later withdrawn. He restored the Parliament dissolved in 2002 in April 2006 amid Jana Andolan.

Shah, Paras Bir Bikram

He is the only son of King Gyanendra. He was involved in a hit and run accident, killing one person. A petition from half a million persons was presented against him to King Birendra, his uncle. He was also present at the site of the Royal massacre in June 2001. He was declared Crown Prince in October 2001 four months after the crowning of his father. He is now chairman of King Mahendra Trust for Nature

Conservation, a post also held by his father before ascending the throne.

Shakya, Karna
He is a well-known tourist entrepreneur of Nepal who started the legendary Kathmandu Guest House in Thamel area and played a leading role in building tourism in Kathmandu. His family owns many other hotels in Nepal.

Sharma, Anup Raj
He is one of the judges of the Supreme Court who declared the Royal Commission on Corruption Control as unconstitutional in February 2006.

Sharma, Rabindra Nath
He was minister from RPP during the Panchayat years and also after restoration of multi-party democracy from RPP. He represented a constituency in the central Terai.

Shrestha, Shyam
He is the editor of Nepali weekly *Mulyankan*, and is allegedly close to the Maoists.

Simha, Bharat Keshar
Simha is a retired general of Royal Nepalese Army who was appointed ambassador to Great Britain by King Birendra. He is chairman of Vishwa Hindu Parishad (*World Hindu Federation*) in Nepal and is supposed to be a close advisor of King Gyanendra.

Singh, Mohan Bikram
One of the best-known Communist leaders, he is ideologically quite close to the Maoists. He is leader of a faction known as 'Mashal'. He is from Piuthan in mid-western hills close to Rolpa where the insurgency had its roots

Singh, Prakash Man

He is the son of late Ganesh Man Singh, a leader of Nepali Congress who played a leading role in ending the Panchayat system and bringing multi-party democracy in Nepal in 1990. He was minister in Prime Minister Deuba's Cabinet from Nepali Congress (Democratic) and was imprisoned on charges of corruption by the Royal Commission, which was later declared unconstitutional by the Supreme Court.

Thapa, Bhek Bahadur

Bhek Thapa has served Nepal in many capacities such as finance secretary, governor of Central (Rashtra) Bank, finance minister and ambassador to the US and India during the Panchayat era and later.

Thapa, Kamal

Kamal Thapa, who is from the RPP, served as minister in several ministries during and after 1990. He was also a member of the government negotiating team during a dialogue with the Maoists in 2003. He was appointed Home minister after the Royal takeover in February 2005. He represents Makwanpur district situated just south of Kathmandu valley.

Thapa, Manjushree

She is the daughter of Bhekh Bahadur Thapa. She has written against autocratic rule by the king and for democracy, notwithstanding her family background as she is also the niece of the COAS, Pyar Jung Thapa.

Thapa, Pyar Jung

He is a commander-in-chief of Royal Nepal Army. He has also been part of the UN Protection Force in Yugoslavia. He is expected to retire in August 2006.

Thapa, Gagan

He is a young activist of Nepali Congress and was imprisoned several times protesting against the end of democracy in Nepal. He became a student activist while studying in Tri-Chandra College.

Thapa, Surya Bahadur

Thapa is an elder statesman of Nepal and was prime minister during the reign of three kings: Mahendra, king Birendra and Gyanendra. He was also prime minister in an RPP-NC coalition government during multi-party system. Although he was the founder-president of RPP he leads a break-away group known as Janashakti Party.

Tripathi, Hridayesh

He comes from Nawal Parasi district in the Terai and is a Madhesi Brahmin. He was trained in Russia. He was general secretary of Nepal Sadbhavana Party. He was appointed minister of forests in 1997. He sided with Anandi Devi faction of NSP which is now part of SPA.

Tuladhar, Padma Ratna

He is a Newar Buddhist from Kathmandu and is known to enjoy cordial relations with the Maoists. He has acted as 'facilitator' in Government-Maoist talks. He has the reputation of being a maverick. He was a minister in the CPN-UML government in 1954 and gave a speech about the right of non-Hindus in Nepal to eat beef that led to large-scale protests. He has led a campaign against compulsory teaching of Sanskrit in schools and also for the right of non-Nepali speaking linguistic groups in Nepal.

Upadhyay, Bishwa Nath

He is one of the architects of the 1990 Constitution. He was Chief Justice of the Supreme Court of Nepal for some time.

Upadhyay, Shailendra Kumar

He was a member of the Communist Party in his student days. He served as vice chairman of National Planning Commission and minister of Foreign Affairs during the Panchayat era. He was one of the founder-members of CPN.

Yadav, Chitralekha

She comes from Siraha district in eastern Terai. She comes from the caste of Yadavs who were granted the status of OBC (Other Backward Caste) in India. She was elected deputy Speaker of the House of Representatives from 1999 to 2002. She also officiated the first meeting of restored Parliament in April 2006.

Yadav, Matrika

He is a member of the Maoist Politbureau and comes from eastern Terai. He is one of the few Madhesi leaders of the Maoists. He was a member of the Maoist negotiating team that was in dialogue with the government in 2003. He was arrested in India in 2005 and was handed over to Nepal where he is imprisoned.

Yami, Hisila

Hisila Yami is married to the Maoist leader Baburam Bhattarai. Her *nom de plume* is Parvati. She is a Newar from Kathmandu valley and is a Maoist leader herself. Her father Dharma Ratna Yami was actively involved in anti-Rana activities before 1950.

Appendix 2

Chronology

November 1950: King Tribhuwan enters the Indian Embassy in Kathmandu and takes refuge there. He is allowed to fly to New Delhi. He is accompanied by Crown Prince Mahendra, his two other sons Himalaya and Basundhara, and Prince Birendra. Ranas declare three-year-old Prince Gyanendra as the new king.

February 1951: King Tribhuwan returns to Nepal and the Rana regime in Nepal ends, marking the advent of democracy. He declares his desire to administer the country according to a democratic constitution to be framed by the elected representatives of the people themselves.

March 1955: King Tribhuwan dies in a hospital in Zurich, Switzerland. King Mahendra ascends the throne.

February 1959: King Mahendra announces a new Constitution, which envisages multi-party parliamentary system of government and sovereignty remaining with the king.

1959: Elections held under the new Constitution leads to two-thirds majority to Nepali Congress. B.P. Koirala is appointed prime minister as the leader of largest party in Parliament.

December 1960: King Mahendra dismisses prime minister B.P. Koirala.

1962: King Mahendra promulgates Panchayat constitution consisting of National Panchayat whose members were elected indirectly and where the Monarch remained most powerful.

1972: Crown Prince Birendra succeeds King Mahendra.

1979: Widespread student unrest in Kathmandu. King Birendra announces that a referendum would be held in Nepal to decide upon the kind of government desired by the people.

1980: Referendum to decide whether people want a multi-party or Panchayat system with appropriate reforms results in a narrow victory for Panchayat.

April 1990: Movement for Restoration of Democracy gathers momentum. Panchayat system is dismantled. An interim government headed by Krishna Prasad Bhattarai is formed including representatives of Nepali Congress, CPN (UML) and royalists.

November 1990: New Constitution is promulgated. Sovereignty is transferred from the monarch to the people. Constitutional monarchy and multi-party are made unalterable features of Constitution.

1991: Nepali Congress wins majority of seats in Parliamentary elections and Girija Koirala is elected prime minister.

1994: Girija Koirala dissolves Parliament and calls for elections.

1994: CPN (UML) emerges as the largest political party in Parliament after elections and Manmohan Adhikari becomes prime minister.

May 1995: Adhikari dissolves Parliament and calls for elections.

August 1995: Dissolution of Parliament is termed illegal by the Supreme Court. A coalition government of Nepali Congress, RPP and NSP is formed with Sher Bahadur Deuba as prime minister.

13 February 1996: Maoists attack police check-post in Holleri, Rolpa, marking the beginning of insurgency.

March 1997: Lokendra Bahadur Chand becomes prime minister of UML-RPP coalition government.

October 1997: Surya Bahadur Thapa becomes prime minister of NC-RPP coalition government. RPP splits.

March 1998: CPN (UML) splits. Girija Prasad Koirala becomes prime minister.

May 1999: Third Parliamentary elections. Krishna Prasad Bhattarai becomes prime minister after Nepali Congress wins elections.

March 2000: Girija Prasad Koirala becomes prime minister.

25 September 2000: Maoists attack police check-post in Dunai, Dolpa and fourteen policemen are killed.

April 2001: Paramilitary force set up.

1 June 2001: Royal massacre at the Narayanhiti Palace results in death of King Birendra allegedly by Crown Prince Dipendra. He is declared king but dies in coma. Gyanendra ascends the throne.

6-13 July 2001: Holleri in Rolpa is attacked. Koirala resigns and is replaced by Deuba.

30 August-November 2001: Three rounds of Government-Maoist talks. Maoists attack RNA for the first time in Ghorahi, Dang. Emergency declared.

February 2002: Mangalsen in Achham attacked by Maoists.

22 May 2002: King Gyanendra dissolves House of Representatives on the recommendation of Prime Minister Deuba.

26 May 2002: Deuba expelled from Nepali Congress.

4 October 2002: Deuba proposes postponing elections and is dismissed by King Gyanendra over charges of incompetancy. King takes over executive power and appoints Lokendra Bahadur Chand as prime minister.

29 January 2003: Government and the Maoists declare cease-fire, decision to declare the Maoists as terrorists is revoked.

28 March 2003: Maoist dialogue team with Baburam Bhattarai as co-ordinator arrives in Kathmandu along with Ram Bahadur Thapa Badal, Krishna Bahadur Mahara and Dev Gurung.

16 April 2003: Government appoints six-member negotiating team with the Maoists under the leadership of Deputy Prime Minister Badri Prasad Mandal.

27 April 2003: Second round of talks between the government and the Maoists.

4 June 2003: Surya Bahadur Thapa designated prime minister replacing Lokendra Bahadur Chand.

August 2003: Doramba massacre.

October 2003: Thirty-seven killed in Bhalubang massacre.

December 2003: India arrests Maoist leaders Matrika Yadav and Suresh Ale Magar and hands them over to Nepal.

February 2004: King Gyanendra addresses rallies in Nepalganj and Biratnagar.

April 2004: Deuba is appointed prime minister again replacing Surya Bahadur Thapa. Political parties organise a street rally against oppression by the king.

November 2004: Women in Dailekh turn against the Maoists.

December 2004: Maoists impose blockade of Kathmandu for a week.

1 February 2005: Royal takeover. King appoints himself as chairman of Council of Ministers and forms a Cabinet with Tulsi Giri and Kirti Nidhi Bista as vice chairman.

February 2005: Deuba arrested on charges of corruption by Royal Commission on Corruption formed by the king.

April 2005: Office of UNHCR set up in Nepal.

June 2005: Maoists blow up a bus in Madi, Chitwan killing thirty-seven civilians.

September 2005: Maoists declare a three-month cease-fire. Government does not respond.

December 2005: Maoists declare one-month extension to cease-fire.

25 November 2005: Twelve-point Agreement between Maoists and Seven Party Alliance.

1 February 2006: Tansen, Palpa attacked by the Maoists. Eleven security men and four Maoists killed.

8 February 2006: Municipal elections held, boycotted by major parties and the Maoists.

February 2006: Supreme Court declares the Royal Commission on Corruption Control as unconstitutional. Former Prime Minister Deuba released.

22 March 2006: Second Agreement between the Maoists and Seven Party Alliance. Proposed Maoist blockade of Kathmandu valley was withdrawn. SPA decides to organise four-day strike supported by the Maoists. The Maoists announce cease-fire within Kathmandu valley.

6 April 2006: Seven Party Alliance organises a four-day strike all over Nepal.

7 April 2006: Maoists attack Butwal and Taulihawa in the Terai.

8-9 April 2006: Curfew is imposed in cities in Kathmandu valley during strike. Crowds defy curfew in several locations in the valley. Four persons are killed during curfew.

10 April 2006: SPA decides to extend strike for an indefinite period of time. Government imposes curfew again.

24 April 2006: King Gyanendra declares restoration of Parliament dissolved in May 2002.

28 April 2006: Girija Prasad Koirala is nominated for the post of prime minister by SPA and is appointed by the king. The first session of restored Parliament is held in Kathmandu.

Glossary

Adibasi   A Sanskrit word meaning indigenous. All tribal groups called Janjatis claim to be Adibasi in the Nepalese context.

Bahun   Nepali word for Brahmin, the highest caste who speaks Nepali as their mother-tongue and live in the hills. Many have now migrated to the Terai. A majority of Nepal's prime ministers between 1950 and 2002 were Bahuns including three Koirala brothers (Matrika, BP and Girija). Bahuns also form leadership of most political parties today. Such Nepali Congress leaders as Girija Koirala, Shailaja Acharya, UML leaders as Madhav Nepal, Jhalnath Khanal, Maoist leaders as Baburam Bhattarai and Prachanda are all Bahuns. Bahuns make up thirteen percent of Nepal's population.

Bahunbad   A term signifying nepotism to perpetuate dominant position of Nepali-speaking Bahuns (Brahmins).

Chhetri
The largest ethnic group in Nepal forming seventeen percent of the population. They form the majority of population in all hill districts in mid-western and far-western hills between Bheri and Mahakali rivers. The Ranas belong to this group.

Dalit
A name used in Nepal and India for repressed classes including such occupational castes as kamis (smiths), *sarkis* (cobblers) in the hills and in the Terai.

Dolpa
Name of a district in mid-western hills

Gorkha
The small kingdom in western hills whose King Prithvi Narayan Shah started the unification of Nepal in 1768. It is now a district with a headquarters of the same name.

Gurkha
Name given to soldiers from Nepal in British and Indian armies.

Gurung
An important tribal group in Nepal which live south of the Annapurna Range in the vicinity of Pokhara. Many have been serving in the British and the Indian armies as Gurkha soldiers.

Janjati
A word denoting such ethnic groups in the hills as Magars, Gurungs, Rais and Limbus in the hills and Tharus in the Terai. Although there is a tendency to call all Janjatis as indigenous (Adibasi), it is not correct as some groups migrated to Nepal only few centuries earlier.

Jana Andolan
Popular movement in April 1990 that led to the restoration of multi-party democracy in Nepal.

Jung Bahadur
The first Rana prime minister in Nepal who ruled from 1846 to 1877 and started an oligarchy of hereditary prime ministers that ended in 1951.

Khas A term used to designate an ethnic group speaking Nepali language consisting mainly of Chhetris.

Khumbuwan The hilly region in east central Nepal containing a large population of Rais.

Kirat People living in eastern hills of Nepal and belonging to Rai and Limbu ethnic groups.

Magar The largest tribal group in Nepal found mainly in the hills of western Nepal. Magars have formed the largest constituent of Gurkha soldiers in the Indian and British Armies and have won the largest number of Victoria Crosses. They also made up a large proportion of the army of Prithvi Narayan Shah who conquered Kathmandu valley. There are many Magar commanders in the Maoist army such as Badal.

Madhise (Madhesi) A term used for groups of people living in the Terai speaking languages other than Nepali who form a quarter of the population of the country.

Maithili Language spoken in eastern Terai of Nepal and northern part of Bihar state in India.

Mashal Name of political party similar in ideology to the Maoists.

Nepal Bandha Countrywide strike organised by political parties.

Naxalite Left wing extremists in India similar to the Maoists in Nepal.

Newars Original inhabitants of Kathmandu valley who created many monuments and works of art and who have highest per capita income in Nepal.

Panchayat A system of government under which Nepal was governed between 1961 and 1990 under which no political parties were allowed and the king was the most powerful figure.

Ranas   Oligarchy ruling Nepal from 1846 to 1951.

RIM   Revolutionary International Movement whose membership includes the Maoists in Nepal.

Rolpa   District in west central hills of Nepal containing a large Magar population where the Maoist insurgency started in 1996.

Sherpa   A group of people speaking Tibetan and practicing Buddhism living in Solo Khumbu district in eastern hills who have become mountaineers and tourist entrepreneurs.

Tamuwan   The word Tamu also means Gurung ethnic group. The Maoists have declared Gandaki Zone in western hills having a substantial number of Gurungs as Tamuwan.

Tharu   People living in the Terai on the foothills of Churia range. They are more numerous in the western Terai from Dang Deukhuri to Kanchanpur who had remained backward till recently.

Thakuri   Caste of Kshetriyas to which the royal family of Nepal belongs.

Bibliography

Newspapers and Periodicals

Adhikary, Dhruba H, American Message from Delhi, *The Kathmandu Post*, 11/3/06.

Bhattachan, Krishnabahadur, Naya Rajyasamrachanako Prastab, *Kantipur*, 8/8/05.

Bhattarai, Baburam, On Moriarty's Pontification, *The Kathmandu Post*, 23/2/06.

Bloomfield, Keith George, Absence of consensus road-map, *The Kathmandu Post*, 24/3/06.

Varadarajan, Siddhartha, US and India part company on Nepal, *The Hindu*, 22/2/06.

Dhital, Manarishi, 'Gahro chha aphnai bichalan chhopna', *Mulyankan April 2006, Chait 2062*.

Dixit, Kanak, Till Kingdom Come, *The Times of India*, 14/11/97.

Nepal Samacharpatra, 24/6/05.

Nepal Samacharpatra, 13/4/06.

Bijaya Kumar, Tito Satya, *Nepal*, 13 April 2003.

Ghimire, Yubaraj, Great Gambler, *The Indian Express*, 29/1/06.

Mahara, Krishna Bahadur, *Janadesh*, 7/6/03.

Royal Proclamation, *Annual Journal*, 2004-5 Nepal Council of World Affairs.

The Kathmandu Post, 19/8/05.

The Kathmandu Post, 8/9/05.

The Kathmandu Post, 9/9/05.

The Kathmandu Post, 3/2/06.

The Kathmandu Post, 10/3/06.

The Kathmandu Post, 7/4/06.

The Kathmandu Post, 13/4/06.

The Himalayan, 8/9/05.

The Himalayan, 17/9/05.

The Himalayan, 7/4/06.

The Himalayan Times, 14/2/06.

The Hindu, 10/5/2005.

The Hindu, 14/5/05.

The Hindu, 10/2/06.

The Hindustan Times, 16/2/06.

Kantipur, 17/4/06.

Jana Astha, 12/4/06.

Leupp, Gary Nepal Pact, *Counterpunch*, 27/11/05.

Bhat, Bhojraj, Kasari khasyo helicopter, *Nepal*, 16/4/06.

Bhattarai, Baburam, On Moriarty's Pontification, *The Kathmandu Post*, 23/2/06.

Gautam, Kul C. Possible Role of the UN in Peace Process in Nepal, *Annual Journal of Nepal Council of World Affairs, 2004-05.*

Ghildiyal, Subodh, Next stop for Red terror: Uttaranchal, *The Times of India,* 17/4/06.

Hilton, Isabel, In cahoots with the King, *The Guardian*, 11/4/06.

Logan, Marty, Nepal: On the Road to Failed State, *IPS*, 6/10/05.

Malinowski, Michael, Maoists are same as Khmer Rouge or Al Qaida, *Spotlight*, 1 March 2002.

The New York Times, 12/4/06.

Philipson, Liz, Negotiating Peace, *Himal Southasian*, March-April 2006.

Raj, Prakash A., China's Nepal Policy, *People's Review*, 6/4/06.

Raj, Prakash A., Maoist insurgency in Chinese eyes, *The Himalayan*, 31/5/03.

Raj, Prakash A., On Prachanda's Interviews, *The Kathmandu Post*, 24/2/06.

Raj, Prakash A., Restoring Peace and Stability, *The Kathmandu Post*, 11/12/04.

Report of UNHCR on the situation of human rights and the activities of the office, including technical cooperation, in Nepal.

Shrestha, Aditya Man, *The Himalayan Times*, 21/2/06.

Shrestha, Ravindra, Janamukti sena maathi Prachanda ra Baburam ko gaddari.

Nepal Samacharpatra, 25/3/06.

Sanghu Weekly, 15/8/05.

Samaya, 19/4/06, Interview with Prachanda.

Sinha, Rakesh Revolution meets confusion, *The Indian Express,* 16/11/05.

Subedi, Surya P. Resolving political crisis, *The Kathmandu Post,* 6/3/06.

Thapa, Manjushree, The Recoup Scenario, *The Kathmandu Post,* 4/4/06.

The Telegraph Weekly, 22/1/2006.

The Telegraph Weekly, 22/2/06, Speech made by Ambassador Moriarty at a programme jointly organised by Ganesh Man Singh Academy and American Center in Kathmandu on 15/2/06.

Books

Dixit, J.N. (ed). *External Affairs: Cross-Border Relations,* Roli Books, New Delhi, 2003.

Enabling State Program, *Pro-poor Governance Assessment in Nepal,* 2001, Kathmandu.

Khatri, Shiva Ram, *Nepal Army Chiefs,* Sita Khatri, Kathmandu, 1999.

Koirala, B.P. *Atmabrittanta,* Jagadamba Prakashan, Kathmandu, BS 2055.

Nepal Tomorrow: *Voices and Visions,* (edited by D.B. Gurung) Koselee Prakashan, Kathmandu, 2003.

Gellner, David (ed), *Resistance and the State: Nepalese Experiences,* Social Science Press, New Delhi 2003.

Mehta, Ashok K, *Royal Nepal Army,* Rupa, Delhi, 2005.

Muni, S.D, *Maoist Insurgency in Nepal,* Rupa and Co, New Delhi, 2003.

Pandey, Nishchal Nath, *Nepal's Maoist Movement and implications for India and China*, Manohar, New Delhi, 2005.

Raj, Prakash A., *Inside Nepal*, Nabeen Publications, Kathmandu 1998.

Raj, Prakash A., *Bahujatiya Bahubhasiya Nepal*, Nabeen Publications, Kathmandu, BS 2056.

Raj, Prakash A., *Dalit Mahila ko Rajnaitik Adhikar* in Jha, Haribansh (ed), Terai ka Dalit ebam Dalit Mahila, Centre for Economic and Technical Studies, Kathmandu, 2003.

Raj, Prakash A., *Road to Kathmandu*, Nabeen Publications, Kathmandu, 1994.

Shaha, Rishikesh, *Modern Nepal: A Political History, 1885-1955*, Manohar, New Delhi, 1990.

Sharma, Prayag Raj, Nation-Building, Multi-Ethnicity, and the Hindu State in Gellner, Pfaff-Czarnecka and Whelpton, *Nationalism and Ethnicity in a Hindu Kingdom*, Harwood Academic Publishers, Amsterdam, 1997.

Thapa and Sijapati, *A Kingdom under Siege*, the Printhouse, Kathmandu, 2003.

The author has given presentations to University of Michigan, Ann Arbor *Michigan*, Michigan State University, East Lansing *Michigan*, University of Iowa, Iowa City, *Iowa*, Boston University Boston, *Massachussetts*, Illinois State University, Normal, *Illinois*, Benedict College, *South Carolina*, Albright College, Reading, *Pennsylvania*, Macalaster College, St. Paul, *Minnesota* and Sweetbriar College, *Virginia* in the United States and Institute of Social Studies in the Hague, the *Netherlands* and University of Vienna, *Austria* in Europe on Monarchy, Political Parties and the Maoists in Nepal that were useful in writing this book.